Motherhood Calling

Experiencing God in Everyday Family Life

To!! Cheryl

you are a treasure
and anointed gift from
God! I hope this brings
you some laughs + spirit.
I hold you + love in my heart
+ prayers always...
abundant Blessings!
Linda
October, 2016

Motherhood calling

Experiencing God
in Everyday Family Life

Linda Anderson-Little

RADIANT HEART PRESS
An imprint of HenschelHAUS Publishing, inc.
Milwaukee, Wisconsin

Published by
Radiant Heart Press
An imprint of HenschelHAUS Publishing, Inc.
www.henschelHAUSbooks.com

ISBN: 978159598-483-8
E-ISBN: 978159598-484-5
LCCN: 2016948637

Cover design by Peggy Nehmen, www.n-kcreative.com
Editors: Bobbi Linkemer, Jody Amato

Printed in the United States of America

For Daniel, Jacob, and Leah—You continue to wow me
with your intelligence, wit, insight, and awesomeness;
I'm so blessed to be your mom!

And for Dan—You are the love of my life
and my best friend; I wouldn't want to share
this adventure with anyone else!

I love you all to the moon and back, always and forever.

The Anderson-Little family
(L to R) Daniel, Jacob, Dan, Leah & Linda

TaBle of Contents

Preface

When I became pregnant with our first child, I was serving in my second church in Kansas City, Missouri. As I learned to pay attention to my body and attune myself to the movement of a new being inside, I was struck by how this process mirrored spiritual listening and discernment. The act of listening to the movement and voice of the sacred within is a different kind of listening from daily conversation, TV-watching, and so on. One has to quiet the surrounding noise, relax the body, and calm the mind; otherwise, it's hard to catch the "still, small voice" of God (1 Kings 19:12). This was the same kind of listening I started doing when I became pregnant, opening a door that brought the spiritual into the physical in a way I had not experienced before.

From that time on, I became more aware of listening differently—not just in my work as a pastor, but also at home in my family life. As our children grew, this practice of listening inwardly was complemented by listening outwardly in a different way as well—to what my children said, to their observations and insights, and to my own struggle to balance the exhausting, high-need stages of child-rearing with my own vocational longings.

The best way for me to integrate my spiritual self with my parenting self and my pastor self—and to express both the anguish and the joy of these sometimes conflicting experiences—was to write. The writing itself helped me to not only name what I was feeling, but also to identify and grasp the deeper movement of God in the daily-ness of life.

I found myself jotting down the things the kids said on the backs of pieces of mail, church bulletins, and old school announcements, including those moments in which I glimpsed a larger meaning. These scraps piled up in my purse or sat paper-clipped together in a drawer until I had a chance to sit down and use writing as a tool for reflection and insight. (Recording what your children say and journaling those "aha" moments is easier now with Apps for our smartphones: check out Kidquoter, StoryCorps, LittleHoots, Posterity, or Limetree.)

In 1999, Morehouse Publishing asked permission to include a litany I wrote in a book called *Women's Uncommon Prayers* (2000), and I began to wonder if maybe this was a sign that my essays could actually be published in a book. For six years, while we lived in Kansas City, I wrote a monthly spiritual-advice column on the religion page of the *Kansas City Star*. Those columns dealt with theological questions, and my essays were about experiencing God in the mess of everyday life. But when I opened that letter from Morehouse, a dream was born.

I wrote whenever I could squeeze it in. Sometimes months would go by with nary a word written, but then we would go to a family camp, where instead of taking an educational course, I would use the time the kids were in camp to write. I would write after I put the kids to bed and Saturday mornings when Dan took them to the zoo. Then there was a long dry spell when we careened from one crisis to the next and struggled to keep our heads above water with body and soul intact.

Over the course of five years, beginning in 2007, both of my in-laws and my mom all had serious, fatal illnesses and died. A favorite aunt, uncle, and grandmother also died. And during that same period, I had very difficult treatment for breast cancer and was on disability for nine months. I could think of things to write, but I could not muster much energy. It took us a couple years before our bodies and souls began to unclench and stop bracing for the next crisis. Slowly, I began writing again, which helped me see that even in the most horrible moments of despair, God held us and carried us through.

My prayer in finally completing this project is that you will view your parenting as a ministry—as a calling—and see all your relationships as sacred places where the holy is present. I hope this book also conveys that children are sources of spiritual wisdom and that, if faith in a higher power means anything, it affirms that all of our lives, especially the difficult and dirty parts, are places where God dwells and calls us to deeper meaning, intimacy, and peace.

For those who don't practice a particular faith, who might be "spiritual but not religious," and yet seek a language for expressing their own experiences of spirituality in daily life, I hope you can find some of those words here.

Introduction

My children have repeatedly taught me that God is in everything, everywhere, including in them, the moments of despair, the times of delight, and the spaces where our hearts and love expand beyond our capacity. These spirit-moments cannot be earned or manufactured; they come as unconditional gifts of love and insight that can only be noticed and received.

This book is a memoir about those spiritual "aha" moments in my life as a mom, when writing became an important tool for me to notice and receive these gifts of grace. I began writing them for myself, to affirm that motherhood was a calling, as much as my call to be pastor and serve the church. I wanted to keep myself open to how and when God would show up in my home, as God has shown up in my work as a pastor. Writing also helped me reflect on how I was changing and who I was becoming as a parent.

You can read this book in any order you like. Rather than organizing my thoughts in chronological order or according to my children's ages, I grouped them around common themes, and each chapter has stories from different stages of our lives. Where you begin reading may depend on where you are in your own life. If your children are getting older and your parental role is shifting, you might want to start at the end of the book with "Letting Go." Or if you're struggling with how you feel about yourself and your changing mom body, you could read the "My Body, Myself" chapter. If the press of everyday life is getting you down, you might find some comfort in the "Holy Grind" and work your way forward.

As I write this, our country is fraught with division, anger, and fear manifested in a presidential election littered with unprecedented inflammatory and disrespectful rhetoric, the murder of police officers who were protecting peaceful demonstrators, and the repeated slaughter of African-American men by law enforcement officers. We witness the devastating effects of institutionalized racism woven into the structures of our society, and of ongoing cycles of violence.

I recently read a simple, wonderful response to the question, "Where is God in the midst of evil, disaster, human suffering, and despair?" The answer was, "Look for God in the helpers." I believe the presence of the holy is in the support, the comfort, the wisdom, and most important-ly, the positive action and justice that come from efforts to multiply goodness and love in the world.

For me to participate in the world in that way, I have found that it makes a difference when I first see God in the details of my everyday life, in my children, in my spouse, in our conversations, and in our tears. When I receive the gift that my children have offered me—to see that God is in everything, everywhere—it gives me the hope and strength to participate in the power of goodness (Godness!) in my community and the world. This is my prayer for you, as well.

Linda Anderson-Little
St. Louis, Missouri, July 2016

~ 1 ~

The Holy Grind

*Daniel, your barf is pink
and my barf is brown!*
—Jacob, age 4

Two Two-Year Olds

Being the parent of a two-year-old can be a frustrating experience, though Daniel is a mellow two-year-old compared to many. One recent morning was particularly exasperating. I was trying to get him dressed, and he refused to put on his clothes. I gave up and went to eat my breakfast.

As soon as I turned around and went into the kitchen, Daniel ran after me saying, "Need help with mine shirt." Relieved that he was finally willing to get dressed, I gladly started to put the shirt over his head. But as soon as I began to do what he asked, he whined, "No" and ran away. He repeated this routine of asking for help—and then refusing that help when it was offered—several times before we successfully got him dressed.

That morning when I arrived at work in the church I served, I went to the chapel to pray. As I was thinking about how frustrating Daniel's behavior was, I suddenly realized as I sat before God that *I can be a spiritual two-year-old.* I do the same thing to God that Daniel does to me. It was as though scales fell from my eyes. God is there like a loving parent—ready, willing, and able to help me, to respond to my issues, to give me what I need, and to answer my prayers. Yet, I often refuse the help when it is offered and run away, whining about my problems and burdens.

What a humbling realization, especially for a pastor. With all of my training and experience, shouldn't I at least be a spiritual six- or seven-year old? The truth is, many times I am not. I began to think about how many times I have prayed to God and then taken my burdens back as I went on with my day. I ask God for answers in dealing with balancing the demands in my life, but I don't stay long enough to hear God's response.

I offer up my worries and concerns about a congregation of only fifty people in a building that seats six hundred, but the ache in my back and soreness in my shoulders reveal that I have not left them in God's care. I am carrying them around with me and refusing God's help. I try to cast on God all my cares about another burst pipe in the basement of the church and the hungry children in the neighborhood, but the times I cannot sleep at night reveal that I am still trying to work out my own solutions, rather than being open to receiving God's solutions.

When Daniel behaves this way, we now have several responses, depending on the issue or need at hand. If it is something he really can do for himself, like pull up the covers at bedtime, he has a choice. If he asks me to do it and then refuses help when I respond, he is left to do it for himself because that's the choice he made. Other times, we wait until he is ready to receive help. Sometimes, he needs to get frustrated enough or cold enough without clothes on before he is ready. Forcing him does not work.

I wonder if God takes a similar approach with us, allowing us to do those things we are capable of doing for ourselves, but willing to provide help when we really need it. Perhaps God waits until we are finally open to receiving help before it's offered. All that is necessary is to *ask*. Why is that so difficult for me?

This summer I am turning thirty-five. Spiritually, I am hoping for three.

Missing the Twos?!

I miss the purity and simplicity of Daniel's two-year-old days. I loved living in his two-year-old world. His doll, which we had bought to assist Daniel with potty training, was simply named Dolly. She was a girl because we couldn't find a boy doll who wet his pants. Daniel would carry Dolly and her bottles upstairs for naptime in the back of his dump truck. In the mornings, he took great delight in putting on makeup with me—eye shadow, mascara, lipstick—and giggling at how great he looked in the mirror. I could refer to God as "she" in our conversations and our prayers and, for him, this was normal.

But now, at three and a half, that pure innocence is gone, and he is beginning to see and conform to the real world. Dolly is at the bottom of the toy bucket; trains, trucks, and Legos are the preferred toys. He no longer puts on makeup with me and, when I kiss him goodbye, he exclaims, "I don't want lipstick on me. Get it off!" When I refer to God as "she," he argues with me. Now that Daniel has spent a year in Sunday school, he knows that God is, in fact, a "he" because that's all he hears at church. Daniel says the Easter Bunny can be referred to as either "he" or "she," but God can't.

The world and the church are already influencing him and countering the values and openness we try to instill. The saving grace is that we can talk about it with him, at least for now, and teach him to think critically about the words, values, and beliefs our society and our church articulate.

Poopland

I have yet to find anything sacred in poop. But every parent I know has a poop story or two of disgusting magnitude that brings raucous laughter when retold because we all know what it feels like to be at the mercy of an explosion from down below.

At first, the "ExerSaucer" seemed like such a brilliant baby/toddler invention, offering entertainment and movement but with containment. It was every parent's dream. It didn't feel like a cage the way the playpens of old did. It didn't require a degree in mechanical engineering to assemble and hang from the doorframe like some monkey swing. It didn't take up three quarters of the living room like a swing with legs.

I could move it to the kitchen when I was cooking, the bathroom when I was showering, the living room when, God forbid, I was using a video or *Sesame Street* as a babysitter so I could have an adult conversation for the first time in ten days. It was complete with rattles, toys, bells, and whistles. You put the legs of your nine-month-old through the holes of the seat, and he had surround-swirl activity at his fingertips. It felt educational and stimulating, it exercised those chunky little legs, and rocked back and forth for comfort when needed. I could add Cheerios to the tray with a sippy cup, and snack time was a snap.

If exercise helps to move the bowels, then this contraption was aptly named. I advise using it for short periods of time and making frequent diaper checks.

My husband and I learned this helpful parenting tip one Saturday morning while we were reading the paper and drinking coffee. Daniel was happily bouncing away in his ExerSaucer when the round saucer part on the bottom looked a little odd. Upon closer examination, we discovered Daniel making poop footprints with his fat little toes all over the bottom of the saucer. With every bounce up and down, he smashed the poop in his diaper, and it squished out the sides in feathery scrolls like frosting from a pastry tube.

The great thing about being a two-parent household in such moments is the ability to share the clean-up and laugh about it later. My husband, Dan, was shirtless, so he took the poop-covered Daniel upstairs to clean him up without smearing the mess on any more clothes. I tackled the ExerSaucer. Thankfully, whoever designed it had the foresight to know that the seat the baby sat in would need to be washed, so I was able to detach it, rinse it, and run it through the washing machine.

Later that morning, Dan went to play racquetball with his exercise partner. They played a few hard, sweaty games, walked several laps around the track to cool down, and then sat in the sauna before hitting the showers. As they sat in the sauna and talked, Dan happened to look down; there was poop in his belly button. Any parent who doesn't believe he or she lives at the mercy of poop isn't really paying attention.

As Daniel got older, we had a "poop stick" by the toilet to break up the big ones so they wouldn't clog the plumbing in our old house.

With our second son, Jacob, who was two years younger than Daniel, there were no poop footprints in ExerSaucers or belly buttons and no need for a poop stick, but there was plenty of obstinacy about potty training. Being in what I called "diaper hell" for seven and a half years— four of them with two children in diapers—I was a little anxious for him to get this potty thing down.

We had a book of blank faces that came with different eyes, ears, nose, and mouth stickers, and each time Jacob used the potty, he could add a sticker to the face and make something truly silly. This was only mildly amusing to him. Much more entertaining was the knowledge that he could tie me in knots at times by not cooperating. Now, that's a funny face worth working for. It wasn't like we rushed the potty training with him, either. We waited until he was three years old—a year after Leah was born—before we even tried.

One fall afternoon, I was running just a minute late from picking up Daniel, now 5 years old, from a French class he was taking. As I was rushing Jacob toward the van, I noticed he had wet his pants while I was putting Leah in the car seat. I had to get Leah out of the car seat and back in the house, call the school and let them know I would be late, and then take Jacob in the bathroom to change his clothes. I quickly pulled down his overalls and his underwear. A huge round turd rolled out of his underwear and onto the bathroom rug.

He had a (pardon the expression) shit-eating grin on his face matched by the twinkle in his eye. I scolded him, which I probably shouldn't have done; I was just convincing him all the more how skilled he was at getting the better of me. Somehow, he knew I lived at the mercy of poop, his particularly.

Leah was easy to potty train. All it took was offering her chocolate if she used the potty, and she was trained in a week. It was getting her *off* the chocolate even after she was trained that was the trick. Once we had Leah, all the "no-sugar, health-food" goals we had with Daniel went by the wayside, especially after the first Halloween.

But during her diaper days, we took a trip from St. Louis to Madison, Wisconsin, to visit Dan's family. In those early years, fast-food restaurants with a play area became a Mecca for us because the kids needed a safe place to run off all their pent-up energy. A rest area with a playground attached *sounds* like a good idea in theory, but one has to have the time to make a lunch after packing all the diapers, baby food, blankets, stuffed animals, toys, bibs, highchair, portable crib, and all the other flotsam and jetsam of traveling with small kids. Plus, promising a Happy Meal with a playland is great bribery for good behavior in the car. (We gave up the notion that we don't use bribery a long time ago; we call it negotiation, sometimes, but who are we kidding?)

On that particular trip, we stopped at a fast-food chain for lunch halfway through the state of Illinois. The kids ate their lunch first, and then off they went. Burn baby, burn; burn up that extra energy. After about twenty minutes, we were getting ready to go. Leah came toddling down the play equipment and over to our table. Something smelled. "Not a poop explosion in the playland!" I moaned to my husband. I looked at the back of Leah's pants and legs; poop was everywhere. Visions of the ExerSaucer popped into my head. Dan checked his belly button.

I did the diaper check to see how bad it was. I pulled back the top of her diaper and looked down past the cherubic cheeks of her behind. Nothing. Oh God. It was *someone else's poop!* Another child had an explosion and left some of it behind, smeared down the slide. The only thing worse than dealing with your own child's poop is dealing with mystery poop. Thank goodness for disinfectant wipes, vans with accessible suitcases, and a sense of humor. Now, we refer to all playlands as pooplands, lest we forget to be prepared for someone's—anyone's—unexpected explosion from down under.

If there is anything sacred in any of our poop stories, perhaps it lies in the willingness to clean up someone else's mess. That is, in short, what we believe Jesus came to do.

Present Anxiety

t's December twenty-first, and I'm in the gift frenzy of the Christmas craze. *Have I remembered everyone? Have I given them enough? Will someone give me something when I haven't give them anything, and will I get that yucky feeling of un-thoughtfulness?* Whoever said it's "the most wonderful time of the year" wasn't in charge of the family gift-giving and never had *present anxiety.*

The teacher gift phenomenon is really weighing on me this year. My younger two children, Jacob and Leah, are at one elementary school, and Daniel is at another one. Here is the teacher gift count to date: with the office staff, nurses, and all the teachers, including art and music, I had ten gifts ready. We passed them out after the Christmas program, and I realized we forgot the gym teacher and the school counselor. Now, we're at an even dozen.

At Daniel's school, it's about the same: hard-working, wonderful people who do amazing work, which add up to eleven more gifts. It's a good thing I run a home business with a skin care and cosmetics company, and can go to my shelf to wrap sugar scrubs, body lotions, and after-shave balms. Yet, at nearly two dozen gifts just for teachers, it adds up, even at wholesale prices.

But here is my dilemma: Daniel, a fifth grader, goes to the middle school for eighth-grade algebra. I was hoping to draw the line at junior high as far as teacher gifts. If I give this one eighth-grade teacher a gift, it feels like opening

Pandora's gift box. Two dozen teachers' gifts for three children would turn into three and four dozen over the junior high and high school years. Leah is only in first grade.

I felt overwhelmed, but couldn't seem to give myself permission to not give the algebra teacher a gift. I asked Daniel. No, he didn't need to give her a gift. I asked my husband. No, he didn't need to give her a gift. He didn't need to give some of the previous two dozen gifts either, but, God bless him, he had the restraint not to tell me so at that moment.

I didn't get a gift together for the algebra teacher, but I still felt uncomfortable about it. It fed my anxiety about other presents. Once I delivered the teacher gifts, I looked at the list. I had put ten boxes in the mail to family and friends, including one birthday present.

Oh, no! I've forgotten the UPS deliveryman, Jeff, who comes to my house regularly, and the mail carrier. Amazed that I had anything left, I pulled something off the shelf to wrap for them later.

Perhaps I could bake pumpkin bread for the neighbors, and what about the children of our former neighbors who have lovingly sent us several Christmas ornaments from our nation's capital? I wanted to send them and their daughter something for Hanukkah. I still needed to get my grandmother's gift and my brother's birthday gift in the mail. Perhaps I could pull something together quickly, pick up a Hanukkah gift, add it to the box, and get to the post office with these last boxes before my 10 a.m. appointment.

I hurriedly wrapped up some cologne. I looked at the table to grab the packing tape and get ready to go. Something was wrong. *Shoot!* I had put the woman's name on the UPS guy's gift. Wow, good thing I caught that; she probably wouldn't want a men's fragrance. I'm not sure UPS Jeff would like *Velocity for Women* either—it has "a light citrus fragrance with a banana flower top note."

I rushed to the bathroom to apply my makeup with this ambitious, frenzied plan in mind to get all this done before 10 a.m. I turned on National Public Radio while I put on my makeup; "Morning Edition" was still on the air. They were doing a story on a former telecommunications executive who retired at fifty-seven but lost half his savings in the dot-com bust in the late 1990s. He bleached his gray beard, moustache, and eyebrows white and went to Santa School with a thousand other men who looked just like him, in order to earn money during the holiday season.

I thought it was kind of sad until I realized he seemed to relish the joy and meaning this job brought to his life, which he didn't have in his previous work. A little boy sat on his lap and whispered in his ear. Santa whispered back. The boy got off Santa's lap and said with glee, "Santa loves me!"

Why couldn't I hear that Santa loves me *before* applying the new ultra, lash-thickening, volumizing mascara? Tears flowed. I looked like a football player ready to battle the opponent and the sun's glare. *Santa loves me.* This one simple declaration on the radio laid bare all of the present anxiety I seem to have every year.

I thought I had outgrown it, dealt with it, gotten over it, and moved on, but the gift frenzy of the morning told another story. The gifts I give and the anxiety I feel are hungering after one simple desire: to be loved. All I need to know is that God loves me, my mother and father love me, my husband and children love me, my extended family and friends love me, the teachers I want to thank with gifts love me, and, indeed, even Santa loves me.

I grew up in a family where feelings were not often openly expressed. I've heard Garrison Keillor of *A Prairie Home Companion* say that we Scandinavians don't talk about the things that are most precious to us—our faith and our feelings. This means that presents carry a lot of meaning because they express our feelings. They are not tokens; they are it.

Love was expressed not just in the gift itself, but also in how it was beautifully wrapped with lovely bows. My mom, who was superb at making each gift special, was on the cutting edge of bow fashion. If the "in" thing was spiked, we had spiked; super curly, we had it; bow gifts, we were the first. We even had a bow maker. My artistic, older sister made beautiful bows and wrapped packages with sharp corners. I never could get mine to look as good; my bows were a floppy mess, and my corners were mushy.

If the gift needed to communicate all the love and appreciation, gratitude, affection, and thoughtfulness I feel toward people, my gifts were always coming up short. Maybe my family wouldn't know how much I love them or see it in this lame bow I've made. Worse yet, what if I find out that they don't really love me? Thus, *present anxiety.* Apparently, it's the gift that keeps on giving. Great.

The simple declaration, "Santa loves me!" from the story on the radio reminds me that I truly am loved before I have given or received a single gift. And this is true even if I don't get the present right, wrap it with sharp corners, or ever make it to the cutting edge of bow fashion.

This declaration of love didn't change my course today. I still went to the store for that last gift, put the package together at the post office, and mailed off my Hanukkah gifts, birthday gift, and the last of the Christmas gifts.

But I kept thinking about the junior high algebra teacher. What did I really want to tell to her? I really wanted to communicate appreciation and gratitude, which I could do by writing her a thoughtful note in a holiday card. I decided that's what I would do for her and anyone else in the junior high and high school who would have a significant impact on my children's education and lives. This gave me a freeing, peaceful feeling.

Hearing that Santa loves me was the only Christmas gift I needed this year. It was God's way of telling me that she loves me no matter what, and I really can just relax and be loved.

To Tease or Not to Tease

The other day, Leah came home from elementary school and recounted how one of the girls in her third grade class said, "I hate you" to her a number of times that day. I listened and figured it was pre-adolescent girl banter. The next day, she came home and said the same thing. I decided to pursue it. She explained to me that the girl said it when she was walking by Leah's desk.

I said, "Well, if I called this girl's mother and asked her to talk with her daughter about this, what would she say was happening *before* she said these mean things to you?"

Leah was mortified. "Don't do that!" she exclaimed, alarmed that I might actually call this mom and cause Leah mortal embarrassment. 'Fessing up to me became the lesser of two evils.

"Well . . .," she started, "I might have said that she and the boy she was sitting next to made a cute couple."

"So, you were teasing her?" I clarified. "What do you think would happen if you didn't say these things to her? Would she still say that she hates you?"

Leah pondered this possibility and thought that she would try it the next day. Sure enough, she came home the following day and said, "I didn't say or do anything today that caused anyone to say they hate me." Breakthrough!

Of course, we don't make or cause other people to be mean; they make their own choices. But learning that our behavior and words create an environment for positive or negative behavior toward us is a lesson I hope my daughter continues to absorb.

It's easy to act like a victim and never take the time to look at our part in a situation. When Leah changed her behavior, the other girl changed her behavior in response. It was the *Serenity Prayer* in action:

> *God, grant me the serenity to accept the things I cannot change, the courage to change the things I can, and the wisdom to know the difference.*

Leah became aware of whom and what she could change and acted on that power to see if it made a difference. Not bad for elementary school. It was a good reminder for me, too.

The Mystery of Feminine Hygiene

One evening as the kids were finishing dinner and I was cleaning up the dishes at the sink, Jacob disappeared from the kitchen and reappeared with something in his open hand. He held it out to me and said, "Mom, what's this?" A piece of purple plastic shaped like a lipstick tube rested in his hand like a wounded bird.

"It's a used tampon applicator. Please put it in the garbage and go wash your hands!"

He stood there looking at it, and then me, and back to the applicator again. "Will you please do as I say and go throw it out and wash your hands? Where did you get it, anyway?"

"I picked it up off the ground on the way home from school."

Daniel shouted out, "It's been in a girl's VAGINA!"

Leah, not yet menstruating, but familiar with the topic shouted, "Ewwww, gross!!"

I realized I was treading on thin ice as far as respect for the female body goes, so I said, "It's not that women's bodies are full of germs, but it's been on the ground. So please, do as I say, and throw it out and wash your hands."

Such is the curiosity of a middle-school boy. Jacob, still holding his prized possession that aroused everyone's curiosity and emotion, said flatly, "I thought that's what it was."

I offered, "If you were so interested to see what it looked like, you could have just asked me, and I would have gotten a tampon and showed it to you. You don't have to pick up garbage on the way home from school to learn about these things."

He didn't respond, but finally threw away his treasure-hunt prize. The very next day, via the Internet and newly released iPad, Apple helped him learn about the advantages of such feminine hygiene—slim, easy to carry, absorbent, user-friendly, and simple to use.

About two weeks later, Jacob marched into my bedroom and said, "Mom, what's this?" Of course, he had a panty liner in his hand. Thank God it was unused. "It's a panty liner."

"That's what I thought," he said, holding it up to his crotch in various positions, trying to imagine how one might use this contraption of feminine mystery. "How do you use it?" I could hear three boys giggling from his bedroom across the hall.

Relieved that he taken me up on the idea of just asking, I pulled a pair of underwear out of my drawer and demonstrated the genius of adhesive protection. "You wear it on light days, either at the very beginning or the very end of your period. Then, you pull it off, roll it up in some toilet paper like this, and throw it away."

(I remembered the parenting instruction to only give the information they ask for, so I did not mention other times of the month when we might want that "clean, fresh feeling." I can be such a talker that I am pleased every time I manage restraint.)

His response: "Gross."

"Where did you get it? You didn't pick up garbage off the side of the road again, did you?" I asked.

"No, I found it in my room, in a bag. What are these doing in my room?" A good question. He brought me the bag, and sure enough, here was the sandwich bag full of individually wrapped pads and several panty liners that he had found on his bookshelf.

At the same time, we solved the mystery. We had a houseguest who stayed in his room a couple of months ago, and she must have forgotten them. Unfortunately, she was related to one of the three boys sitting on Jacob's bed, snickering at this unusual find.

We thought a little harder. My sisters and mom had also visited in the fall for a girls' weekend, and they could have left them behind, which we decided was a more likely explanation to spare his friend embarrassment.

Jacob walked into his room, and like an expert in all things gynecological, explained how the panty liner worked and that they were used for "light days." I popped my head in and enlightened his friends about our "girls' weekend" and how someone must have left them behind. For now, all things are right in the pubescent boys' world.

From Spitting Up to Just Spitting

I think I can survive every stage of parenting—except the preteen and early teen, very male stage of "hawking loogies." Give me wet dreams, sheets to launder every night, cussing, Internet issues, dating, driving, even a night at the ER with a broken collar bone—but please, spare me another Sunday breakfast like the one I had this morning, complete with bagels and loogie-hawking off the back porch.

We were a bit pressed for time, as usual, scrambling to get breakfast and make it to church without being late after the twenty-five-minute drive. I was busy trying to get everybody's bagel prepared just how they wanted it: white versus wheat, toasted versus untoasted, butter versus cream cheese, cut up versus whole. They all had their own special preferences, which required different preparation and sadly, I had already been catering to these individual needs too long to stop this morning.

Invariably, I got someone's breakfast wrong: "I said I wanted the wheat bagel!" said Daniel indignantly.

"How was I to hear this request above the all hawking and spitting?" I replied, with thinly disguised sarcasm in my voice. "You're snorting it up and coughing it out; Leah and I are screaming at you to go outside; you leave the door open; we're shouting at you to shut the door; Jacob is having spit-target practice from the doorway and hitting the deck rail; you're asking me if you can spit out the van window when your distance gets better. HOW am I supposed hear a request for a wheat bagel in the middle of this loogie-fest?"

He gave me a wry smile. He knows I'm right; yet, he finds the whole loogie-content of the morning and my exasperation with it quite amusing. I start the process over with the wheat bagel: toasted, buttered, and diced, so it doesn't break off a wire in his braces. Jacob keeps going out to the porch to hawk and spit. Leah and I keep yelling at him to shut the door. Oh, to live in a city that's not the allergy capital of the country. Then I would just have bagels and picky eaters to deal with, but no loogies.

We left for church, leaving bagel bites scattered on the kitchen table like so many jigsaw puzzle pieces. Another grand maternal effort at fairness, pleasing, and nourishment—wasted. All I got in return for my efforts were a lot of loogies.

Yesterday we were driving back from swimming lessons and Daniel, sitting in the front passenger seat, decided to hawk a loogie out the window. Only he missed, and it whipped back in and stuck to the window frame.

"That's it!" I yelled. "No more spitting from the van!"

"Mom, it's not my fault!" Daniel insisted. "We turned just then; if we weren't turning, it would have been fine!"

"Well, that's just too bad. I have loogie limits," I told them. "You will discreetly use a paper towel if you must, and hold it in your hand until we get out of the van. Then you will throw it away in a trashcan. Next time you spit from the van, it will cost you $5!"

Of course, the question came, "What if we don't have $5?"

"Then I'll take an advance out of your babysitting money." That is what he receives when Dan and I go out now that Daniel is old enough to stay home with the other two. Even Jacob and Leah get some money for behaving, though not as much as Daniel; that way, everyone is invested in making it work.

But they're kids, so they never leave it alone. They had to ask me this morning if their aim got better, could they start spitting out of the van? Do they think I took a stupid pill? Like I'm going to say yes to that and have them practicing off the back porch every morning. Actually, it probably is my fault since I let them know it bothers me. I have given them the power to gross me out and irritate me at the same time. It's the perfect preteen combination.

The best I can do with them now is to lay down the law and then appeal to their interest in girls. Hawking loogies is not the way to win girlfriends and influence admirers. So far, this strategy is not working since it's summer, and there are no girls around to impress—just boys on the block, boys on the baseball team, boys on the basketball team, and boys at church. Boys who like to spit.

Who knew I would pine for days of milky spit-up, clothes that smelled like rotten baby food, sleepless nights, and sore nipples? I couldn't control those little baby eruptions either, but there is something sweet and innocent that is lost when spit-up turns to just plain old spit.

Dan is not really helping my cause. We left the house late one afternoon recently for a spur-of-the-moment date. Our kids were visiting a friend who offered to keep them for dinner so we could go out. It was a thrilling moment. We left the house in about six minutes to catch a 4:30 movie and then go to dinner. We held hands just to walk to the car; we were so excited at this serendipitous opportunity. Dan dropped my hand just past the door, walked a few steps ahead of me, and spit. At least he apologized, but I almost turned around and walked back in the house.

I deal with this all day. I finally get a night out with my husband, and what's the first thing he does? Is this genetic or something? Part of the male DNA? It's hard for me to convince the boys that they won't get girls to like them when their father does it and he already has me. Unless they don't think of me as a girl one wants to get . . . but let's not follow that train of thought.

Usually, one can get backup from the quintessential man, the fully human, but also fully divine—Jesus—when looking for the model of decent behavior. But I find I am not getting much help there, either. The man spit, and it's recorded in Scripture. Granted, he did do it to heal people, not to win a loogie-hawking contest (although maybe he did that, too, and they just didn't record that part. Anyone who uses saliva for healing just might be interested in that sort of thing.)

The most well-known healing-with-spit story is the healing of the blind man in John 9, when Jesus made mud with his saliva in the dirt and put it on the blind man's eyes.

Jesus told him to wash in the pool of Siloam and when he did, he could see. In another story in Mark 8, Jesus heals a blind man just with saliva, without the mud and the washing in the pool.

A lesser-known healing story that involves spitting is recorded at the end of Mark 7, when a deaf man, who also has a speech impediment, is brought to Jesus for healing. After Jesus puts his fingers in the man's ears, spitting and touching his tongue, the man's ears are opened and his speech restored. No wonder it's lesser known! I would rather have spit-made mud on my eyes than someone's spit right on my tongue—even Jesus' spit.

There is no talk of loogies, thank goodness, only saliva. But my question is: why did Jesus go there at all? There are plenty of healing stories, including when Jesus heals the blind and the deaf simply with his touch. No spit at all. He could have just left the spit out of it and given moms like me an opportunity to say, "'Thou shalt not spit!' It's the eleventh commandment, recorded in the book of *First Hesitations*. Jesus didn't do it, so you can't either."

It's moments like these where my gender-neutral assumption about God goes right out the window, and I think, "God really must be male. There are so many little things he could have done to make life just a little easier for women, and he blew it."

Here's another example. There's the healing of a blind man in Mark 10 and one in Luke 18, where touching wasn't even involved, just words: "Your faith has made you well." If touching is enough in some cases, and just words and faith are enough in others, why open the spit can?

Maybe I am the only person who has researched how the words spit, spits, spitted, spat, and saliva are used in the Bible. But, in every instance other than for Jesus' healing, spitting communicates disgrace, shame, and exclusion of another person from the community, at least for a period of time, like seven days. When a woman's husband died, it was the man's brother's duty to marry her and continue a family in his brother's name. If he refused, the woman would spit in his face as a sign of shame and refusal to carry out his family and communal duty.

Before Jesus was crucified, the Gospels of Matthew, Mark, and Luke all record that Jesus was spat upon, in addition to being beaten and mocked as a sign of his shame. The blind, the lame, the deaf, and the mute were also disgraced members of the community. They were unclean and, therefore, unable to enter the gates for worship or to live as a part of the community. Being spat upon would not be an uncommon experience for them.

So why heal them with spit? Perhaps it was to do some symbolic jujitsu with the prevailing culture of shame. Jesus took a symbol of shame—being spat upon—and turned it into a vehicle for healing and restoration. He didn't need to do it every time, just often enough for it to be noticed and recorded. Such action embodies the great reversal of which Jesus spoke: *The last shall be first, the first shall be last; those who spit in the face of the lame and the blind shall be humbled, and the spat upon shall be healed and honored.*

Shoot. I guess that trumps a mom trying to get her boys to stop spitting. I suppose this means I can be grateful they don't spit *on* anyone. But you can bet I won't be mentioning the healing angle of spitting, or we will be into a whole conversation on the healing nature of hawking loogies versus swallowing, especially when one suffers from allergies. God forbid they would try to heal someone with their spit. I wouldn't put it past them. I will just have to stick to the argument that there are no loogies in Scripture, and there is no hawking from the van unless they also want to cough up five bucks. Oh, and call the allergist.

~ 2 ~

Children's Spiritual Wisdom

I know why they have a cross on this hospital.
So when people who are really sick and
dying will see it, they'll remember that God is
always with them and they won't be afraid.
—Daniel, age 5

Literally

The first several Sundays after I resigned from full-time parish ministry, I attended the church where my husband served. I kept Daniel, then nearly three, with me in worship, rather than sending him to the nursery with his younger brother, Jacob. Before each part of the service, I whispered to Daniel what we were doing, especially as we sang the hymns. Right before we sang, I gave him the words so that he could sing along with us.

On the first Sunday we did this, I made an amazing discovery. During the processional hymn, "We Have Come into This House" as we sang the third verse, "Let us lift up holy hands . . . ." Daniel lifted up his hands to act out what he was singing. After the confession and forgiveness, we sang, "Glory, Glory, Hallelujah," and on the second verse we sang, "Feel like shouting, 'Hallelujah' since I laid my burdens down . . ." and Daniel did it again. He shouted, "Hallelujah" as he sang, rather than saying it as the rest of us did in a bland tone that communicated we were about as excited about God's forgiveness as we were about wet toast.

Daniel took the hymn words literally! What a radical concept. I wonder what kind of church we would be if we all took the words of our hymns literally.

"Now thank we all our God, with hearts and hands and voices . . ."

"Dance, then, wherever you may be, I am the Lord of the dance, said he . . ."

"We have no mission but to serve, In full obedience to our Lord; To care for all without reserve; And spread his liberating Word."

"Lift ev'ry voice and sing, Till earth and heaven ring, Ring with the harmonies of liberty."

"We give thee but thine own, Whate'er the gift may be; All that we have is thine alone, A trust, O Lord, from thee."

"Jesus loves me this I know, for the Bible tells me so. . ."

Daniel has given me a vision of a church that is dancing, praising, singing, grateful, serving, giving, praying, liberating, loving, and transforming. All we have to do is *do* what we sing.

Real Fish, Real Jesus

We were driving home from our first week of swimming lessons at the beginning of summer. Daniel announced that he wanted fish for supper. "It will make me swim better," he said, explaining the rationale for his request. When we got home for lunch, I asked my husband (the grocery shopper and cook at the time) if we had any fish sticks in the freezer because Daniel wanted fish for supper.

Upon hearing this, Daniel urgently said, "NO! I want REAL fish. REAL fish will make me swim better."

We chuckled and went on with our meal and our day. But in the back of my mind, I thought about what he said. Eating fish—the best swimmers—would help him swim better, but only if it were *real* fish and not the reconstituted frozen stuff.

Suddenly, it dawned on me why we Lutherans are such sticklers for believing in the *real* presence of Christ during the Sacrament of Holy Communion. How can we live and act more like Jesus if he's not really present and we're not receiving the real thing? We have to take in Jesus to behave more like him in the world. We do not eat Jesus in a cannibalistic sense, of course, but he is present and enters us spiritually "in, with, and under" the earthly elements of bread and wine. REAL presence.

Daniel is not even four, yet he has a sophisticated theology of Holy Communion and a better understanding and rationale for it than most adults I know, including me. And yet, many would exclude children from the Sacrament because, "They don't understand it."

Thanks to this three-and-a-half-year-old child, I now understand it better than ever.

The Suit

While "casual Friday" is sweeping the nation in dressing down corporate environments, Jacob, at age three and a half, has been swiftly debunking the whole philosophy before our very eyes. We don't know how long it will last, but he is in his "suit phase" of attire. I'm not sure how many parents are dressing their son for preschool by getting out a pair of khaki or navy-blue dress pants, usually reserved for Easter Sunday, Christmas Eve, and weddings; a white button-down shirt; a clip-on tie; a sport coat; and the children's vinyl version of wing-tip shoes one can find at Target around the holidays. Who knew?

Something happened to Jacob on Easter Sunday when he donned his Easter best, and I'm not sure it had anything to do with Jesus rising from the dead. Maybe it had more to do with the fact that when he dressed like this, he got a lot of candy. Or perhaps it was that a lot of adults paid attention to him and talked to him like he was the cat's pajamas. Somewhere in Jacob's little mind, he decided this was a trend he would like to continue.

So, when we packed for a trip to visit my parents in Texas after Easter, we tried to include some sensible play shorts and shirts, sandals, and tennis shoes for the running around we would be doing. Jacob, however, insisted we pack *The Suit*. Believing some freedom of expression in personal style is an important value, and that this may be the only time I would see my son willingly wear a suit, I went along. I wasn't entirely certain he was going to wear it anyway.

Sure enough, we arrived at my parents' house and dressed for a hot day of exploring Dallas, and Jacob insisted on wearing *The Suit*. The rest of us were dressed in shorts and tennis shoes.

Despite our protestations about how warm it would be, Jacob was convinced, right down to his wingtips, that this was the outfit for him. Away we went, to explore the Dallas Farmer's Market, see the elaborate electric train display in the front of the children's hospital, go out to lunch, and visit other sites around Dallas with two parents and two kids dressed for vacation and one three-and-a-half-year old ready to trade on the stock market.

Jacob knew exactly what he was doing. He had all of Dallas eating out of his hot little hand. Strangers—from moms and grandpas to cowboys and wing-tipped business-men—were coming up to Jacob and talking with him about his dress, his style, where he was from, his shoes, how he liked Dallas, and so on. Jacob loved every minute of the attention he had purposefully attracted to himself by the way he dressed. He chatted people up, flashed them a devilishly cherubic smile while sweat glistened between the hairs of his crew cut, and kept on strutting until the next passerby took notice of him.

We stopped for lunch at a restaurant near the hospital to get some Texas burgers and fries. Even while we were sitting at the table, people would stop and talk to Jacob. Standing, walking, or sitting, Jacob was a billboard advertisement for the simple truth that how you dress affects how people treat you.

Now, granted, he was a little kid dressed like an adult, which is a bit unusual. But the basic principle is the same, which is why we have dress codes in professional environments. We subconsciously treat someone who is dressed professionally with more respect and trust than we do someone looking like he just rolled out of bed and slept in his sweats. We are more likely to let the former, rather than the latter, prepare our taxes, invest our money, write our wills, sell our homes, counsel us, and so on.

Wearing *The Suit* not only affected how people treated Jacob, it affected the way he behaved. He didn't run around quite so much. He carried on more adult conversations. But the quintessential moment when I realized how much our dress affects our behavior was when we went to a park later that afternoon. He was not ready to change into shorts, even for the playground. Are you kidding? After the stellar day he had?

So, off we went to a playground full of swings, slides, monkey bars, and a climbing apparatus that went in every direction. Jacob decided to tackle the slide the first. He climbed up the steps slowly, careful not to slip; the suit jacket restricted his arms from easily reaching out and grabbing the poles on either side of the steps as he climbed up the back of the slide. He reached the top, got himself seated, and down he went with that big grin on his face. His wingtips hit the rubber shavings, he stood up and, in one smooth motion, he tucked his tie back into his jacket (which was still buttoned), left hand on the lapel, right hand smoothing down the tie. Then he marched to the back of the slide and did it over and over and over again. Every time he went down the slide, he stopped at the bottom to tuck his tie back in. Those waiting at the top of the slide had to wait until the tie-smoothing ritual was complete before Jacob would step out of the way.

Jacob continued to wear *The Suit* to preschool for quite a while that spring. In fact, it became quite a trend, and a few of the other boys started at least wearing clip-on ties to school. Thankfully, he didn't wear his jacket every day, so he didn't have to tuck his tie back in every time he went down the slide at recess.

I have never been a great fashion maven or always up on the latest trends. I am guilty of having pooh-poohed the significance of clothes, appearance, and presentation in the past, arguing that a person's substance and personality are much more important. Of course they are. But I must admit that Jacob has changed how I get dressed in the morning.

I've decided I want to do my best to help others see my substance by paying closer attention to how I package it. Now, whenever I think that how I dress for the day is not going to affect how I behave, a picture of Jacob tucking in his tie at the bottom of that slide pops into my head. I think about what I want to accomplish that day, how I want to be perceived and treated by others, and then I get dressed.

It's okay to leave my pajamas on until noon if I don't want to get anything done, and I just want to hangout and relax. But, if there's a lot to do, even if I'm just staying at home, then I must get showered and dressed for success with my makeup on.

I want to put my best effort forward each day in using the gifts God has given me and, if The Suit is going to help me do that, well, so be it.

The Ministry of Presence

I sat on the floor playing a game with Daniel. We finished and his attention turned to puzzles, which he can very easily assemble on his own. I saw my opportunity to get some dishes done and seized it. I got up to go into the kitchen, but Daniel tried to stop me: "Mommy, stay with me."

Wanting to get some housework done, I responded, "But you can do those puzzles all by yourself. You don't need my help."

Without missing a beat he quipped, "But you can help me by watching."

Aha. Parenting is a "ministry of presence." He didn't want my help; he wanted my presence, my being-ness, my attention. We in the clergy love to talk about and engage in the "ministry of presence"—being with people in times of need. We do not necessarily offer great words of wisdom or comfort, but our presence reassures them that they are not alone, that we struggle with them, that we care about them and that, therefore, God does, too.

I have never questioned the need or validity of spending hours with a family at the bedside of a critically ill member, at a funeral home visitation, or on pastoral visit in a time of major stress or change. I don't leap up and rush off to the tasks of ministry as soon as they give me an opening. I stay with them until it is clear that the pressing moment of need has passed, or someone else is there to offer support.

Then I find a way to complete the tasks of ministry, be it a newsletter article or going through the mail, making calls, or preparing a sermon. And if there isn't time to complete the tasks well, most will wait until next week because the more important ministry of presence has been fulfilled.

But the moment my son engages in an activity he can do on his own, I leap into action to complete the tasks of daily living. Daniel is much less concerned about a clean kitchen than he is about my presence with him. Daniel is less interested in whether the carpet is vacuumed and much more interested in whether I am sitting on it with him, focusing my attention on him. It's not that I can be there all the time, or that the housework doesn't need to get done. He does need to learn to play on his own, and dirty dishes do need to be washed. But perhaps I could approach my mothering more like my ministering.

Parenting is a ministry of presence—something that is more important than the tasks of homemaking. Housework will always wait for me to get to it. But like ministry, parenting has opportunities and moments that don't and can't always wait. My prayer is that, next time, Daniel won't have to ask me to stay.

Box Canyon

M ost summers, we go to a Presbyterian conference center in northern New Mexico called Ghost Ranch. It's in the high red-rock desert at about six thousand feet of elevation, and the scenery is stunningly beautiful. Georgia O'Keefe lived on ranch property and made this area her home, painting many of the mountains, rocks, and flowers in her magnificent artwork; she also created the logo for the ranch itself.

The routine of the ranch works well for pastors with families who need to satisfy both continuing-education credits and family vacation time. Classes are offered every week in the summer; and while adults are learning or taking an art class, the children are in day camp. Classes and kids' camp run 9:00 a.m. to noon and 7:00 to 8:30 p.m. for five days, with the afternoons free for family time.

My favorite part of the arrangement is that we all eat in the dining hall; aside from clearing our trays and bringing them to the dishwashing area, there is no cooking or dishes for a whole week! Heaven on Earth! It's amazing how much time this frees up. The camp is open to everyone; no religious or spiritual orientation is necessary—just a love of the outdoors, a love of hiking, or the desire to try a new skill or class.

The ranch is complete with a pool, two small museums, a library, horse stables, hiking trails, high-and-low ropes courses, kayaking at the lake across the road, a nurse, a gift shop, and a great photo opportunity in front of the cabin built for the movie, *City Slickers*, part of which was filmed there.

Our week here was going better than it did the last time. Leah was now four and a half. Actually, last year, she and I stayed home while Dan took the boys to the ranch because the year before—when Leah was two and a half and first eligible for day camp—was a little stressful. She didn't want to be left at day camp, she kept wetting her pants, it was hard to keep track of her racing around the dining hall, and my food was always cold and accompanied by indigestion. So, I must modify my sales pitch for this place and say that this is the perfect vacation for families with children ages five and up.

We were planning to hike a trail called Box Canyon as a family. It was to be a warm-up hike to see what Leah at almost five could handle. The prior year, when Dan came alone with the boys, Daniel at nearly eight and Jacob at almost six, conquered Kitchen Mesa, a much more difficult hike, so Box Canyon was going to be more like a walk in the park for these veterans of Ghost Ranch hiking. Slathered in a fresh coat of sunscreen, hats to hold the heat of the afternoon sun at bay, and water bottles in our backpacks, we set off.

We had just walked around the bathrooms by the casitas where we stayed and headed up the hill toward the hogans, traditional New Mexican dwellings, when Leah tripped on a rock and landed on all fours. She fussed a minute but didn't cry. She got up, brushed off her knees, and caught up with her brothers at the top of the hill. I wondered how this hiking venture might go. Would we make it all the way to the box-like canyon at the end of the trail? Would a family hike on the harder trails, like Chimney Rock or Kitchen Mesa, even be a possibility with the newest hiker in our clan?

But once we got on the trail, Leah attacked the task at hand like she does most things—with a dogged determination and independence that both delight and startle me. She loved traipsing along, holding her daddy's hand, safe, yet freed from my overprotective impulses. After being helped across the first *arroyo* (creek bed) by her dad, Leah decided she could do all the others on her own.

"I can handle it!" became her Box Canyon motto. Leah asked for help only when the leap across the mud was longer than her little legs. She scrambled across rocks, balanced on the often-narrow paths, leaped over the creek, and gave her older brothers a run for their money. Leah always loved to feel things—worms wriggling in her hands, mud oozing between her fingers, water bugs floating in the pools of creek water, and the feathery softness of small, native flora.

About halfway through the hike, we paused to look up at the great cliffs that stood like sentinels above us. The yellow, orange, and gray rock shimmered in the heat of the afternoon. In a deep crevice near the top, we spotted an enormous nest with branches and twigs jutting out from the rock in a tangled mass—the home of a golden eagle couple. I tried to imagine the first fledgling flight of an eaglet three months after hatching in this aerial home: fly or die seemed like the only options for these fierce creatures.

I watched Leah assert her ability and independence as she scrambled up a boulder ten times her size. I had no doubt that we would make it to the box-shaped canyon at the end of the trail.

"She is relentless," I said to Dan. I can still hear the echo of her voice reverberating off the canyon walls as she yelled out her victory at the end of the trail. Yes, she's going to follow the eaglets and fly.

Dance Like Nobody's Watching

After five years in St. Louis, we moved to a new house to ease some financial strain and live in a different school district. We moved in the fall and, by January, I wanted to enroll Leah, then four, in a dance class. Unfortunately, the class had started in the fall, and while it was fine for her to join, they had already purchased their costumes for the spring dance recital, and it was too late to order one for Leah. We decided that was okay and if she liked it, she could dance in the recital the following year.

I didn't anticipate how sad I would feel, however, when the costumes arrived, and it was time for dress rehearsal. The girls were dressed up like honeybees with black-and-yellow-striped dresses and hats, black tights, and shoes. Even though they were only in preschool, the rule of the studio was that hair had to be pulled tightly back and makeup perfectly applied.

The other eight girls in the class were all glamour, color, and taffeta, and there was Leah, pale-faced and wearing her light pink leotard and tights. My heart ached for her to be so out of step with the rest of the class.

After everyone's hair and makeup were checked, it was time to practice the dance. I prepared myself for a meltdown, a refusal to dance, or a crying jag for not being included in the costumes and recital. What a bummer she learned a dance nobody was going to watch her perform.

I have never been more wrong.

Leah pranced out there like she was the star of the show. She seemed to dance with more verve, greater joy, and a bigger smile, as if to say, "Who needs a costume to dance your heart out?"

I watched her shining face, the playful flick of her wrist, the perfectly timed swaying of her hips, and the tapping of her feet as tears streamed down my cheeks.

It was my problem, not hers. I wanted to have a meltdown and a crying jag and be mad at the studio for not finding a way to get Leah a costume and include her in the recital, and I had projected my feeling onto her. I didn't need to remind her to go out there and still do her best; I needed to remind me to be my better self.

At age four, she already knew that it wasn't about the performance, the recognition, or the glamorous costumes. You dance because it's fun, and the music is on! Joy and integrity are inside jobs, and she showed up with them even when nobody was watching.

On the day of the recital, Leah and I dressed up and made a date of it. We went out to dinner first, and then went to the show. We cheered on her classmates and congratulated them when they were done. I felt blessed that my daughter taught me how to handle it.

~ 3 ~

Feminism and Motherism

Are we God's toys?
—Leah, age 4

Indispensability

I was driving home from a hospital late one night after spending about seven hours with a family whose teenager had been severely injured. I began to wonder again why God had called me to this ministry of part-time, on-call chaplaincy, something I started to do shortly after I left the congregation I had served full time.

I had asked the same question of my spiritual director a couple weeks before. *Why does God want me here? Am I being prepared to deal with the serious illness or injury of one of my own children?* These were thoughts that had occurred to me more than once. *What was I supposed to learn from this calling, which was both similar to and quite different from my eight years as an urban pastor? Just what was God up to?*

My spiritual director looked puzzled and responded, "Perhaps you are just there to help people through a terrible situation, and that's all. You are there to minister to them in the moment. Isn't that enough?"

Apparently not, since I kept asking the question in the back of my mind. There must be some spiritual discipline, some larger meaning to my chaplaincy ministry, some insight I was supposed to glean. As I drove, my thoughts returned to the time I spent with that family and the significance of what they were enduring.

I had been with them while the surgeon spoke to them before and after the surgery. I held the weeping mother as the doctor offered a grave prognosis. I walked with the family back to the patient's room and stood by them as they each witnessed this young life hanging by a thread. I offered fervent prayers, reassured them of God's presence and love for all of them, and shared information with the family's pastor when he arrived.

It was the most traumatic event in this family's life, and God used me to help them through the initial crisis. When I left the hospital, I filled out my report, passing the pastoral baton to the full-time chaplains who would pick up the case in the morning.

That's the hard part for me. After eight years as a parish pastor, I don't do any follow-up or ongoing care. I will never see this family or most families with whom I minister ever again. Of course, that's what enables me to spend time with my own children; the job is limited in scope and time. The full-time chaplains take care of follow-up.

Then it hit me. I needed a larger meaning, and so God gave it to me: the spiritual lesson was that, as a pastor, I am not indispensable. There were other chaplains, other pastors, family members, church members, and a local community that would provide a network of support for this family and others. It was not only me; it didn't have to be me who would provide all that was needed.

As with Elijah, God is always able to call forth other faithful people who can carry on the ministry. While this seems to be stating the obvious, it's hard for those us conditioned with hyper-responsibility to see—with an "if it is to be, it's up to me" mentality.

This has been one of my primary struggles in urban ministry—the feeling that I am the only one responding to overwhelming needs. At the hospital, God uses me in the moment of immediate need and will use others in the ongoing moments that follow. I am not alone. What a liberating realization after years of feeling, however inaccurately, that if I didn't do it, no one would.

I am indispensable, however, when it comes to being the mother of Daniel, Jacob, and the new life growing inside me (Leah). If something happened to me, they would surely survive and thrive, but I am their only mommy. I think I have often behaved as though these roles were reversed—as though I were indispensable in my job, but dispensable to my family.

God has given me the opportunity to get my spiritual values straight—to be the one and only mother to my children and part of the "priesthood of all believers" who care for people in crisis.

Grandparenting

When I first began to "supply preach" (substitute for another pastor) after resigning from full-time ministry, I found the experience pretty frustrating. Preaching for me was so connected to being part of a community that it seemed to underscore the feeling of being disconnected from every congregation in which I found myself. I missed the ongoing relationships with people who shaped the preaching event, and I would come home feeling somewhat hollow and empty.

Then, I took a break from supply preaching for about a year. The month before Leah was born, I stopped accepting invitations to preach, wanting to wait until she was about three months old to return to this occasional work. At that time, we had moved to St. Louis with three children under five; in fact, we had moved twice in three months (talk about chaotic). First, we moved into an apartment and then into our house, once we found it. A few months after we moved into the house and achieved a modicum of order, I accepted a new preaching engagement.

Something had changed inside me in that year, but I was unaware of it until I preached again. I had the time of my life with the congregation that morning! It was so much fun to preach and lead worship, to officiate at a Baptism, and to preside at Holy Communion. I enjoyed every minute of my time with the people of that church. But, I also loved being able to get in the car and drive away.

As I drove home, I thought about what had changed. *Why was I having so much fun now, when the same thing caused me pain a year ago?* Then it occurred to me, as if the Spirit were whispering in my ear. Supply preaching is to full-time ministry what grandparenting is to parenthood. I get to come in for a short period of time and have fun with the congregation. I can give them candy (with some nutrition, of course), enjoy being with them, delight in the experience, and when they get upset or complain that this is not the way they have always done it, the responsibility is not mine. I can hand them back, having had a good time and earned a little money. So, I get the pleasure without the sometimes unpleasant responsibility that goes along with it.

It seems somewhat odd that I have become a grandparent in my vocation so that I can be a parent in my family. I do have ultimate responsibility for my children—fussy moods, messy diapers, complaints, and all. Maybe a year of just being with them has given me the peace I need to enjoy the opportunities I have to use my skills.

I know deep down it is too difficult for me to have the ultimate responsibility for a congregation and for my children, at least while they are small. For now, being a grandparent in the former enables me to be a more faithful parent in the latter.

Bottled Up

This is one of those weeks when I just want my own life back. Perhaps it is an illusion, but I want that feeling again that I am the master of my own destiny, the determiner of my day. I want to have my own thoughts, uninterrupted; my own projects accomplished, or, if unfinished, left undisturbed on the table where I leave them. I would like what is put away to stay put away, what is cleaned to stay cleaned. I'd like to be able to put my glass of water on the coffee table without one of my kids coming by and pouring it on the carpet. I'd like to have a quiet cup of coffee in the morning without having to get up at the butt-crack of dawn to get it. I would like to feel useful in the world and important in someone's life in a way that does not include cooking, dishes, laundry, cleaning, or driving.

Is it too much to ask to feel like my own person—a person who has an important existence beyond making everyone else's life work? That's the problem with the transition from full-time career to full-time mom. It has been difficult to go from being a messenger of God's love and grace at significant moments in people's lives to keeping track of show-and-tell days and making class treats. Maybe I need to think of show-and-tell days and class treats as moments of God's love and grace for my kids, but, on many days, that's a stretch.

It seems my sole purpose now is to do all the mundane tasks of life, enabling everyone else in my family to go about his or her life's purpose while I feel lost in the middle. What about my life's purpose? It was so clear to me when I was a full-time pastor. Now it seems muddled.

A member of the church where my husband is the pastor has become a good friend of mine. She shares similar struggles staying home with her two boys after working in nonprofit management. She said when she hears me lead Bible study, preach, or teach at church, she's surprised because she knows me as a mom. Then, she says, "I wonder how you stay at home with all of that bottled up inside you."

I wonder how many moms are at home with the gifts and talents they have to share with the world bottled up inside of them. I'm fortunate in that I can let mine seep out once or twice a month with substitute preaching and teaching a monthly women's Bible study. I realize how important it is because, without it, the pressure would just keep building inside, like nursing breasts being squished by a toddler who just wants to "push your buttons" (as Jacob says) so you might forget about that darn baby and older brother. Or like a soda can that has been tossed around and shaken up. It just comes spewing out when you finally open it, making a big mess rather than quenching anyone's thirst.

Perhaps it's not my calling that has changed, but the way in which it is served—in sips, rather than a big gulp. For now, for this time while my children are small, perhaps a sip is enough for me and for others and for God. That is, after all, what we receive in Holy Communion. A sip is enough for grace to be full.

A Kidney Stone
Does Not Equal Childbirth

I farted while walking out of a fancy Indian restaurant after having enjoyed a very nice lunch with Dan. (It has taken me a while to actually write this!). It wasn't one of those SBD farts—silent but deadly—that anyone could have let slip out. Had it been, I could have discreetly walked out and no one would have been the wiser. Fortunately, I was walking toward the door, so I just kept on going and marched down the street like the businesswoman I appeared to be.

Only one couple remained in the restaurant. Maybe they thought it was the server who was straightening the table near the exit. I hoped so, because I talked to that woman when we intersected in the hallway near the restroom, and I got her name and phone number so I could call and give her a makeover. I looked so sharp that day, too. I wore a bright blue suit, matching scarf, and coordinated jewelry; my curls were coiffed to a professional, yet fun, look. Even Mary Kay herself would have approved of me. Until my heel hit the ground a little too hard as I rushed to catch up with my husband, and there it was—the fart that announced my departure.

I didn't even know it was there, lying in wait, like a leopard hiding in the bush waiting for the precise moment to pounce on its prey. Little did I know that my put-together

-having-a-fabulous-day-getting-new-names-for-my-business-having-a-rare-lunch-out-with-my-husband-looking-great-self was the prey this secret fart was after.

I haven't been able to call that woman and book her for a facial because I'm afraid she heard it and thinks I'm the lady in the blue suit who farts. It's a good thing I didn't sneeze, or I would have peed, too. It's the new postpartum form of multitasking. If I would have dropped something and bent over, all hell would have broken loose.

My husband, Dan, thinks that because he had a severely painful kidney stone land him in the emergency room once, he has experienced the equivalent of childbirth. This argument doesn't wash with me. He was given drugs that completely knocked him out. He got to sleep through it once they diagnosed him. When it came time to pass the stone, all he had to do was pee into a strainer. The stone was like a large grain of sand. This is nothing like a nine-pound baby or the two eight-and-a-half pounders who followed. I like the former Robin Williams' suggestion in one of his comedy routines: "Guys who want to know the pain of childbirth can try to 'open an umbrella up their ass.'"

But let's say for the sake of argument that the pain of a kidney stone is equivalent to the pain of labor. Dan does not live with the long-term effects of childbirth on his body. Passing a tiny pebble has not stretched out his urethra or his ass. I don't hear his gastrointestinal tract ambushing his professional image. I don't see him leaking when he sneezes. In fact, I don't see him multitasking at all.

I discussed this loss of lower extremity control with an ob/gyn at a dinner party celebrating the Mexican holiday, the Day of the Dead. Dr. Kim is perfectly comfortable discussing anything, anywhere, so I sat next to her and picked her brain. I asked if Kegel exercises would help with the suck-up-ability factor with gas-passing. With her hands dancing in the air above our plates, like finger puppets in the shapes of vaginas and anuses, she explained that Kegels wouldn't help if there was an inner tear, but that surgery could repair it, and bladder surgery could fix the leaking problem.

An anal tear was a real possibility for me since my first child, the nine-pounder, wouldn't descend into the birth canal and was sucked out with a vacuum extractor, during which I tore all the way to the rectum—and during which my epidural didn't work. Forty-five minutes of stitching me back together may not have repaired me just right.

Some others at the table, medical professionals all, including Dr. Kim's husband, looked askance, obviously thinking, "Oh my God, she's talking about anuses at dinner!" I convinced them that I had asked her about this topic, and it really was okay. Although, I did empathize with their discomfort when I looked down at our plates and remembered our chicken was swimming in chocolate brown mole sauce.

Dr. Kim's personal and medical conclusion was that we each have to decide what our limit is, what is tolerable for us and what is not. She herself had bladder-repair surgery, although in her case it was related not to childbirth, but another medical issue. Her deciding moment was when she and her husband were at a party and she had had a little too much to drink. They were dancing the polka and laughing, and she was peeing across the polka floor.

My fart didn't seem so bad after hearing that. Another friend, with whom I can discuss this taboo topic, shared that jumping on a trampoline after two beers was another non-postpartum activity. Bring an extra pair of pants or a bag of Depends if you decide to try this at home, or worse yet, at your neighborhood block party.

We could decide to polka under the influence, trampoline after two beers, or go about our business in our bladder-stretched, anus-torn world and just put up with the inconvenience as we gush about how these beautiful children made it all worth it.

Or, we could decide to have surgery to repair our stretched and torn parts. Would insurance cover it? Surely it would qualify as a medical necessity. I would like to hear my doctor explain why the need to stop peeing and farting while I'm really trying to walk, unload groceries, attend a parent-teacher conference, run a business, and live my life is indeed a medical necessity. How bad does it have to be?

My husband doesn't live with any of these problems. Drinking enough water solves his problems; drinking too much creates mine. Peeing solves his problem; peeing creates mine. Which brings me back to my original point: a kidney stone does *not* equal childbirth!

~ 4 ~

My Body, Myself

*Mommy, why do you have all of this
extra blubber on your legs?*
—Jacob, age 7

To Linda, From Linda

In an old episode of *Star Trek Voyager*, Ensign Harry Kim makes a mistake that kills the crew of *Voyager*, and he spends the next fifteen years trying to go back in time to fix the problem. Finally, through a time disturbance, Harry is able to correct his mistake in the past and change the course of events. In doing so, he sends a message from fifteen years in the future back to himself on *Voyager*. The message was called, "To Harry Kim, From Harry Kim."

Just a few weeks ago, both my husband and my spiritual director, independent of each other, asked me to engage in a similar exercise—to send a message to myself at age eleven—when I was a chubby preteen with freckles and braces who thought she looked like a pig in her school picture.

Why, at age thirty-six, a mother of three, a pastor for more than nine years, married for eight, did I need to talk to myself at age eleven? Several issues converged at the birth of Leah, our third child and first daughter, creating a crisis in my body image and sense of attractiveness.

After three children, my body was no longer what it used to be. Getting out of the shower in the morning caused a lot of turmoil. All I could see was a stomach that still looked six months pregnant, varicose and spider veins decorating my legs like a map, and once-perky breasts making a sagging slide toward my protruding middle. Surely my husband would have no desire for me now and would at least want to look at women more beautiful and desirable than me.

After weeks of painful struggle, the issue finally became clear. It was not that having three children made me unattractive; it was that I have *always* felt fat, ugly, and unattractive. I had been masking and covering up the pain such feelings caused since I was eleven years old.

Tears cascaded out. I felt so sad for that little girl who thought she was ugly, who looked at her picture and thought she looked like a pig. I cried tears of grief that anyone would feel about herself as she did and despair that she had spent twenty-five years carrying around a hidden feeling of shameful ugliness that was really based on a lie. Someone should have told her the truth—pastors, parents, teachers, aunts, or uncles—but no one knew she needed to hear it, or perhaps they would have spoken up. Or maybe they felt ugly, too, or pained in some other way, which blinded them from seeing what she needed.

Having a positive body image became harder when hurt was added on top of pain. No one asked me to the high school prom. My mom tried to comfort me by pointing out that I was so tall, and that in high school boys wanted to date someone smaller. Maybe this would change later on.

When I was in college, a male relative said to me, "You should lose weight and grow your hair if you want to date." That was bad enough, but on my wedding day, he came through the receiving line and self-righteously quipped, "See, I told you all you had to do was lose weight and grow your hair," as if that were the only reason I managed to snag a husband (who wasn't intimidated by a tall woman—my mom was right, after all!).

When I saw my grandmother two months after Leah was born, she commented that she never wore leggings because she thought her butt was too big. "But," she said to me, "you're wearing them and your butt is a lot bigger than mine" (and I'm so glad I spent eight-and-a-half hours driving with three kids under age five on Christmas Day to hear that!). The painful memories go on and on.

That eleven-year-old girl needed to hear the truth, and maybe that could help redefine those later experiences for her. I was the only one who could tell her what she has always needed to hear. So I wrote to her.

To Linda at age eleven, from Linda at age thirty-six:

Dear Linda,

I'd like to tell you that you are beautiful just the way you are, that God made you just the way God wants you to be. There is no one standard of beauty, but God instills beauty in every creation. We each carry our own unique beauty, which God gives us to show the world. God gave you beautiful blue eyes, a radiant smile, wonderful freckles, and wavy reddish hair. You are tall and strong and perfect just the way you are.

I'd like to tell you that people love imperfectly. I know people have said hurtful things to you about your body and your looks. It's not that they want to hurt you or don't care about your feelings. It's that they are imperfect. They hold their hurts and insecurities and pains inside, and sometimes these feelings come out in hurtful ways. But their unkind comments are about them, not about you. They are not a reflection of your value, worth, or beauty as a person; they are a reflection of how much they hurt and feel insecure inside. They love you, but all human love is flawed. That's why you must only look to God as the source of that perfect love you seek. Only God loves perfectly and without inflicting pain.

Every person, regardless of how much he or she loves you, will hurt you or fail you at one time or another. Only God's love is perfect. When you truly believe your value and worth as a person comes from God and not from what anyone else thinks or says or does, then your beauty will really shine forth and be recognized by everyone who meets you.

Let them go. Let the nasty comments and the negative thoughts go. Cancel them out in your mind and heart. March up to the mirror and tell yourself you are beautiful; then, go share your unique beauty and personality with the world. Clearly, it needs you."

Love,
Linda

I can't put myself on a new timeline and erase the past, like Ensign Harry Kim did on *Voyager.* I cannot regain the time and energy wasted over the last twenty-five years of feeling fat and ugly. But I can change how I feel about myself now and in the future. I can opt for God's view instead of the world's view. I can also think differently about my past.

Rather than hang on to the pain I've been carrying for so long, I can let it go—not just the pain at age eleven, but also in the many years that followed, when these feelings were dominant. I can let go of shame. I am grateful, for through giving birth, I am the one who is being reborn and given a new life.

Plastic Surgery

I am embarrassed to admit how often I think about plastic surgery. Just about every morning when I get out of the shower. A tummy tuck here, a liposuction there, a nip of the dropping eyelid that is folding its way to toward my eyelashes. Cascading flesh giving in to the relentless pull of gravity. I look at the folds of skin resting like a turned-down bed atop my mother's eyes, and I wonder how long it will take me to apply eye shadow when the inevitability of my genetic makeup and age catches up with me. Perhaps the Mary Kay image won't be so important to me then. On the other hand, maybe it will be more so, and plastic surgery will not feel like an excessive luxury, but a vocational necessity.

Perhaps I wouldn't think so much about plastic surgery if I had not sat next to a plastic surgeon at a church dinner shortly after Dan was called to serve as pastor of a church in St. Louis, Missouri. The doctor was one of St. Louis' best with the knife—not just cosmetic surgery, which was only about a quarter of his practice—but with the real healing work of reattaching hands and closing with fine stitches the gashes that have torn open flesh in the harshness of life. This doctor alluded to free procedures for the pastor's wife with the comment that I could come into his office, and he could, "fix me up."

I had inquired about the goiter-like wattle of flesh that hung below my not-yet-forty-year-old chin. He said that I would just have to wear a strap around my head and under my jaw for a couple weeks after an in-office procedure. Hmmmm. How do you keep plastic surgery a secret with a get-up like that? I was thirty-five pounds overweight—baby fat I had not yet lost from my third and last pregnancy. I vowed to myself that I would lose the weight, do the best that I could do with what I had, and then consider his offer.

Well, I lost the weight more than a year and a half ago, but my four-year battle with chronic and severe migraines pushed to the background the thought of undergoing a painful procedure. But recent progress in my treatment had shifted my attention, and plastic surgery once again filled the obsessive vacuum. I imagined not only the possibility of fixing all of these imperfections I have learned to loathe about my body, but also fixing them at a price I could afford. The American woman's dream: body beautiful within my grasp. I was a normal weight, quite a feat for my body type after three babies, but it was much harder to lose a life-long fat mentality.

I pressed my hands against the outside of my thighs and pictured them straight up to my hips. No more rhino haunches for me. I turned to the side and pulled my leg skin upward. The hills and valleys of dimpled fat my body was too stubborn to burn disappeared for a moment. Is this what the prophet Isaiah meant by "making the rough places a plain?"

I turned forward again and imagined a new stomach pulled taut and flat. I wondered what my new belly button would look like—an innie or an outie? The white and pink spaghetti junction of stretch marks that circled my lower abdomen would be gone forever.

It was a tantalizing thought. With bare, flat, taut, and pierced midriffs staring at me from every billboard, magazine, TV commercial, and Internet pop-up site, I have yet to see one marked by birth, along with the caption, "How beautiful upon the abdomen are scars of the one who brings forth life" (to misquote Isaiah 52:7).

My ob/gyn told me that the rounded bulge at the bottom of my belly would be my constant companion. Regardless of how many sit-ups I did, this "mommy-pouch," as she called it, would never go away. *Great. Now I am a marsupial.* I lifted my arms in the mirror and waved them with verve. The mud flaps of flesh that hung where triceps used to be waved back at me.

I had been doing both sit-ups and push-ups at least three times a week to improve this mommy-pouch, mud-flap situation, honoring my vow to do the best I could with what I had. I looked vainly for progress from my efforts, but all I could see was the flapping and hanging skin of an aging body.

I realized my skin would never regain its elasticity. It was like a rubber band that had been stretched one too many times, and it just sat there with a limp, wavy edge. I pushed my breasts back up to where they used to be in college, when someone had actually called them "perky." That was before I nursed three children and they stretched and shrank, stretched and shrank, and stretched and shrank. Now they have a low-hanging water balloon quality, but I must say, it doesn't stop my husband from feeling me up every chance he gets.

My mother ended up having surgery on her eyelids, a medical necessity because they were beginning to impede her vision. I thought of the plastic surgeon I met, but, alas, it was too late. He was no longer practicing his craft. Perhaps this was better, because it invited me to ponder a more productive path of obsessive thought.

Why not try gratitude for all my body has allowed me to do? Obsessive gratitude might lead my body to respond differently to the exercise routines and disciplines I undertake. It might decide to muscle up a little here and tighten a little there if it actually felt appreciated. Disliking my body has gotten me nowhere, but perhaps I am old enough and mature enough to try total acceptance, aging and all.

Maybe one day I can afford a personal trainer, but I don't imagine hiring one any time soon. Who needs one to have a healthy exercise routine and learn acceptance? Psalm 139 reminds me to praise God, for I am "fearfully and wonderfully" made.

Find a friend and go on a walk or join Curves. I did both. One thing living with chronic pain has taught me is that there is no medical treatment that can replace genuine self-care or any magic pill that beats self-love. As I have grown in both ways, my health, my weight, and my self-image have improved as well.

I am far from the image of body beautiful in the media. It does help to be married to a man who can say that, sure, all the images we are bombarded with are attractive, but they don't make him less attracted to me.

"I'm not married to a billboard; I'm married to you. I want you in your body, not someone else," he says. God bless him for this gift. But I want to provide this reassurance for myself, because there is nothing more beautiful than a woman who accepts herself and feels comfortable in her own skin.

Hot Pink Babe

My *shorts are too tight today*, I thought. So is my shirt. Thank goodness my camp nametag covers the gap that pops open between the buttons.

After twelve-and-a-half years of marriage, Dan told me recently that I was always wearing "frumpy" shorts. This particular day was an aberration from the norm. I happened upon a pair of short pink shorts at Upscale Resale made by a designer I really like. I hadn't noticed their non-frumpy quality. I bought them because they fit, they were bright, and the price was right.

I will admit these shorts showed I had lost the third-and-last-child pregnancy fat. The day I first wore them, Dan panted after me like a dog in heat. That's when he shared his frumpy feelings the pink shorts had unlocked. I also found out about all the other garments that carried the unacceptable "frumpy" label.

After three pregnancies and the extra thirty-five pounds to lose each time, the tent style of clothing was to be purged from my closet forevermore. Dan turned forty in March. He had just gone to the eye doctor and was told he needed reading glasses, now that he was older. Somehow, these events were not unrelated in my mind.

I shared this at a small book group with female friends, at least one of whom also struggled with this issue of dressing for her husband. Our resident psychologist enlightened us: Men are photo-erotic; that is, they are aroused visually, thus explaining the far greater amount of pornography for the male audience. Women, however, are tactile-erotic, aroused by touch rather than sight. The paraphernalia sold in sex shops is designed for female shoppers.

"Dressing younger—'de-frumpified'—is not only arousing, but it also makes the middle-aged husbands feel younger than they are," she added. *Ahaaaa.* Light bulbs flashed around the room. So much for book study.

Dan pondered these new insights, but insisted there was more to his newly middle-aged manhood. Most men, of course, have had a "hot babe fantasy," but at this stage of life, Dan craved the deep intimate connection he had with me. Since he already had what he really wanted, he would like our relationship to integrate all of the varied parts of who he is—hot babe included—which is thankfully, directed toward me.

The pink shorts were the only pair that survived the purge of my summer wardrobe. I had never shopped for tight clothes before. I shared my husband's middle-aged "frumpy revelation" with the sales clerk. A silver-haired woman shopping nearby quipped, "It doesn't get any better!"

I bless the designer who added three percent spandex to cotton. I can sit. I can breathe. It's cheaper than a convertible.

Labyrinth

About four months after moving to St. Louis from Kansas City for Dan to accept a new call at Trinity Presbyterian Church, I attended a feminist gathering of Presbyterian clergy and lay women. The gathering was an opportunity to learn and experience praying the labyrinth, something completely new to me.

The congregation where we met created a labyrinth in the front lawn outlined in bricks—a project facilitated by the leader of the program, Elizabeth O'Neil. She had just completed seminary, where she had learned of the prayer labyrinth, and it had been a significant part of her spiritual development and insight.

Elizabeth shared her own experiences and explained how the labyrinth worked. Many people confuse it with a maze, but it is not a maze; there is one clear path to the center and one clear path out. It is designed to bring clarity, not confusion; release, not entrapment. Walking to the center of the labyrinth is a process of shedding, of letting go whatever it is that you need to release. You pray about what is bothering you, whatever it is.

The center of the labyrinth is a place of waiting and receiving what God has to give you. You can sit or stand there as long as you like. You may receive a clear message, or you may just stand in peace in the presence of God. When you are ready, you come out of the labyrinth, walking with God, integrating the experience and insight of the labyrinth into who you are.

I was still in the midst of what was the most painful and difficult year of my life. I was going through all of the major life changes on those stress charts, in addition to dealing with other significant issues. We had moved three months after our third child was born—twice in three months with three children under five. I hated moving because my family had done so every four years when I was growing up. As a result, old, unresolved emotions from my past were erupting. For the first time, I was entering a new church as a pastor's wife, instead of as the pastor, and struggling with the question of why having children so radically affected my life, but not my husband's.

I was disconnected from my own Lutheran church and missed some of the worship practices. Dan and I were in the painful process of redefining our marriage (and ourselves) after my resignation from full-time work and wrestling with the full impact of children on our marriage. I was having a crisis of body image and attractiveness after my third pregnancy, and the one thing I did for myself while staying home with our children—running a Mary Kay business, which I had built to one hundred customers in Kansas City—had to be restarted in St. Louis.

I felt like I had lost everything—my vocation, my church, my business, my home, my marriage, and myself. The passage from the book of Revelation, "Behold I make all things new" kept running through my head; but instead of a promise, it felt more like a cruel joke.

I told Dan one day that it would be easier if we could just cut open my arm and pour out the blood (like Nicholas

Cage's character in the movie *Moonstruck*). At least it would be quicker and probably less painful than dealing with all this change and loss. A little melodramatic, I admit, but it indicated how much grief I felt. I couldn't give up one more thing, because I had already given up everything.

With all this weighing on me, we went outside to pray the labyrinth and then came back together to share our experiences. It was nothing short of miraculous. I walked to the center, reviewing all of these losses and burdens, as well as the pain and struggle of the life transition I was experiencing. When I arrived at the center, this Scripture passage popped into my head: *When you are in Christ you are a new creation. The past is finished and gone. Everything has become new!* (2 Corinthians 5:17)

Aha. God was making me into a new creation inside and out—a creation defined by God and not by me, the church, the role of pastor, the culture, the Protestant work ethic, the media, nor the swimsuit edition of *Sports Illustrated.* "Behold I make all things new" came to me as well; but, for the first time, it came as promise and opportunity, celebration and hope, rather than burden and sacrifice. It was as if God were fulfilling the promise that, indeed, all things *do work toward good for those who love the Lord and are called according to his purpose.* (Romans 8:28)

The pain, grief, loss, and confusion I felt were not irrelevant to God, but the very place God was creating something new and—not just good, but great—something better than it's ever been. It wasn't that the struggles of this major transition were over, but that I had been given a sense of hope in the midst of it. God was *with* me and *for* me, enabling me to move through the transition toward wholeness and healing.

As I walked out of the labyrinth, I wanted to skip and dance. I couldn't remember the last time I felt really good about being me, and I actually felt like celebrating being me. God was celebrating me. Jesus was walking with me, so it was okay to feel good.

While we shared our experiences back in the meeting room, God gave me one more gift. We sat in a circle and during the course of the entire retreat, my chair faced the tabletop display about the labyrinth, complete with pictures of different labyrinth designs around the world. For almost three hours, the circular patterns of the labyrinth were directly in my view.

One of my body-image issues involved my stretch marks. I hated these scars of pregnancy and resented their ugliness. They pushed me yet another step away from our culture's norms of beauty; they even go above my belly button. I know several women, including my own sister, who don't have any. How did I get so lucky? I tried to remind myself that so many women want to have children but cannot and would give their right arm for the opportunity to have stretch marks, but I still didn't like them. Even though my ob/gyn reassured me that stretch marks were my "badge of honor," and I agreed with her intellectually, I was having a hard time embracing that the Indy-500-speedway of circular stretch marks around my gut were anything but awful.

As I listened to the other women, a dawning came over me: *the stretch marks that cover my belly were shaped like a labyrinth!* I sat and stared at the pictures of the labyrinth that morning long enough that the similarities became undeniable.

My children had given me a form of prayer on my own body. When I was not near an actual labyrinth, I could trace the pattern on paper with my finger and pray the same way. Or in my case, I don't need a printed labyrinth because I can trace it on my own stomach! If our bodies are truly the temples of the Holy Spirit (1 Corinthians 3:19), then I could, at that moment, see mine as a unique house of prayer. God really was making me a new creation.

~ 5 ~

Terror

It's not fair that Grandma is sick.
I didn't even get to know her before!
—Leah, age 6

Paradise Lost

It was one of those rare, perfect Saturdays. Dan had no church duties, and no one was dying at the hospital where I served as an on-call chaplain on the weekends. We had an unusual lazy morning, drinking coffee, reading the paper, letting the boys run around and slide across the room on the shiny magazine-like newspaper inserts. Even hearing a *Barney* video for the millionth time didn't seem to grate on us that morning.

A fresh blanket of snow outside our frosted windows gave us that cozy winter-wonderland feeling. Daniel, who was three at the time, had received his first sled for Christmas the month before, so it seemed like the ideal day to break it in and take the boys for their first real day of sledding.

We bundled them up in their hand-me-down snowsuits from cousins who live in Wisconsin. Thank goodness for older siblings with kids and the small fortune they have saved us in clothes and coats! Jacob, sixteen months old and butterball chubby, looked like a blue mini-Michelin-Man with big, rosy cheeks that bulged out of his hood, tied like a bonnet under his chin. Ever fearful of ear infections, I put a hat on over the hood; the poor child could barely move, much less turn his head or sit on a sled.

Daniel wore green snow pants with a matching jacket. His red knit hat had four fuzz balls on top that bounced everywhere when he moved.

We headed off to the park where there was a modest hill and lots of space. Not many people were there, but we had the best time, watching our sons' faces full of glee as they slid down the hill. One of my favorite pictures of the boys is from that day. They were ready to slide down the hill on the sled, Daniel behind, holding onto his little brother. Their round, shining faces burst from the bundles of coats and hats—exuberant, expectant, ecstatic—soaking in the wonder of snow, sled, speed, and sun that combined for one shining moment of glory.

When it was time for a break, we built a family of snowpeople, with the snowmom holding a snowbaby. Dan found an empty beer bottle (not a surprise in a city park) and gave it to the snowdad to hold, just for symmetry. We went sledding down the hill a few more times, admiring our snowfamily as they watched over us.

When we were pooped and cold, we bade farewell to the snowpeople and headed home for lunch and naps. We warmed up with soup and sandwiches, regaling in the fun of the morning and the boys' first sledding adventure. Then it was up to bed for naps. The boys share a room, but for naptime, we put Daniel in our bed so that they would actually go to sleep. Jacob cuddled up in his crib, and Daniel gave up his racing car bed for the afternoon and climbed into our bed. Within minutes they were both asleep.

Dan and I took advantage of the respite from constant activity to work on our painting project in the playroom on the main floor. It was right at the bottom of the stairs, so if Daniel woke up, we would hear him as we stenciled a train full of circus animals at chair-rail height around the room.

After about an hour or so, I thought I would run up and check on the boys. Jacob was still snoozing away. I glanced in our room, expecting to see Daniel doing the same, since we had not heard a sound from him. The covers were pushed back, and the bed was empty.

"Daniel is not in the bed!" I shouted downstairs to Dan. There were only two rooms upstairs. I scooted around the rooms, looking in the closets, the bathroom, under the beds, and in the shower stall, calling out his name.

Dan ran up the stairs, "What?" he asked, looking at me like I was the crazed, paranoid, overprotective mother that I truly am.

"Daniel is not here. He's gone. Where could he be? We were right there at the bottom of the stairs. How could he come down without our hearing him?" My mind was starting to race everywhere I did not want it to go, along with my heart.

"He must be in the house somewhere," Dan reasoned. "We'll find him."

We ran back downstairs and searched the house, calling out his name. I tried hard not to let the floodgates of panic open up and scream and cry like a maniac on a rampage, but that was how I felt inside. He wasn't downstairs. We ran to the kitchen. The back door was ajar. *Oh, God. Oh, God. Oh, God.* Dan went to double-check the basement; he could have gone out and come back in. I ran outside. The backyard is fenced in and the gate was closed, but he wasn't there.

How long had he been up? How long had he been gone? We lived on the corner of a very busy street. The backyard gate opened to the side street. I ran out to the side street, down the length of the house to the corner in the front where four lanes of cars, two in each direction, were racing up and down at thirty-five miles per hour. What was he wearing? Blue pants and a red shirt. There was no sign of him anywhere. *Oh, God. Oh, God. Oh, God.* My three-year -old was gone. I didn't succumb to hysterics only because I had a toddler in the crib upstairs.

I ran back in the house, hoping against hope that by some miracle, Dan had found him asleep in a closet in the basement. He had a bleak face as he tied his tennis shoes.

"I don't see him anywhere outside" I blurted out, shaking like a dead leaf in winter. "Should I call 911?"

"No," Dan said. "Just wait a few more minutes. I'm going to go look for him."

Wait a few minutes? I thought. *Is he crazy? What are a few minutes? How will he find him, when I was just out there and didn't see anything? How can I wait and not do something?*

As a hospital chaplain, I know all too well what happens to toddlers or preschoolers who walk out the door without their parents knowing. They fall into holes in the street where there are construction sites, but no workers, and they die. They walk into traffic and get hit by a car. Or worse: they fall victim to child molesters or kidnappers, or they just disappear without a trace.

Because I'm too stupid to think about locking the back door during naptime. Clearly, it's necessary even when we're right there, two parents in the room at the bottom of the stairs, two parents with very good hearing, one with "mommy hearing." I hear a cough, a footstep, a whimper, from a dead sleep. *How could I not hear a three-year-old on the stairs in the middle of the day?*

Fortunately, Jacob helped break my destructive train of thought by crying. His nap was over, and it gave me something to do while I followed Dan's suggestion to wait. It's no surprise that Jacob woke up. Perhaps he would have awakened anyway, but with the frantic energy pulsating through the house, we would have aroused the dead.

I picked him up and put him on the changing table. I tried to focus my thoughts on what I was doing. He did not need a mother who was hysterical and totally freaking out. I coached myself through changing a diaper, just to focus my thoughts away from catastrophe.

Pull off the tabs, remove the wet diaper, wipe his bottom. Lift the legs, scooch the clean diaper under, secure the tabs, pull up his pants, smile, and talk to Jacob. You can do it. All the while, I prayed frantically, *"Please, God, protect Daniel. Bring him back to me,"* over and over and over.

As I walked downstairs with Jacob in my arms, Dan walked in the front door with Daniel's hand in his. I put Jacob down, dropped to the floor in a puddle of tears, and I hugged my child like my life depended on it. I have never known relief so sweet, so deep, so agonizing as I did in that moment. And gratitude. Not every lost child is found. Not every parent gets a second chance.

Gerald, a neighbor who lived three doors down and whom we had never met, was walking Daniel up to the house when Dan had gone out looking for him.

"I'm so glad you're not a child molester!" I said to him, shaking his hand, introducing myself, and thanking him profusely. It was the strangest compliment I had ever given and probably the oddest introductory greeting, but never has one been more sincere and heartfelt.

Our parent educator and pediatrician both concluded that Daniel went sleepwalking that afternoon, so he did not make any noise coming down the stairs. Something about the exhaustion of sledding and the deep sleep that came afterward combined to result in this isolated incident. He walked out the back door and probably climbed over the gate. He walked in his stocking feet down the sidewalk in the snow, turned left at the corner and followed the sidewalk, not crossing the street, crying in his sleep, asking for his daddy.

Gerald is a jazz cellist and was getting ready to go to work for the evening. He was loading his cello into his car and saw this little boy walking alone down the sidewalk, without a coat, crying, with his shoes in his hand. The boy seemed in a bit of a fog, but Gerald managed to engage him in conversation, during which Daniel woke up.

Gerald asked him if he knew where he lived. Daniel replied, "6101 Rockhill Road," which was just a few houses up. Gerald took Daniel into his house out of the snow to help him put his shoes on, so he could walk him home. That was about the same time I ran to the corner, seeing neither hide nor hair of them. When Dan went out to look a second time, Gerald was walking Daniel up to the house.

Small miracles along the way prevented this from turning into an absolute tragedy: Daniel knowing his address at age three and being able to recite it when asked, despite his distress and disorientation; Daniel turning the corner and staying on the sidewalk rather than trying to cross the street; Gerald being outside at just the right moment, loading his car; waiting one more minute before calling 911 and engaging the police to help find our lost child.

We ended up getting to know our neighbors three doors down. It turned out Gerald and his girlfriend, Leslie, were engaged and planning to be married but had no one to officiate at the service.

"I'll do it!" I volunteered, "for free!" It was a small gesture I could make in return for rescuing my son, for saving me.

I heard someone say recently that being thankful is to be glad that something happened, but to have gratitude is to want to give something in return.

I worked at creating a service that reflected Gerald and Leslie; it was an act of profound gratitude. The wedding was held in the living room of Leslie's parents. Their staircase became the bridal aisle, and Leslie's twin daughters led the way down to the circle that would form their new family. As I watched her girls begin the service, I marveled at how often, without even meaning to, our children lead us into whom we are supposed to be. On this occasion, the pathway was one of joy instead of terror.

Daniel, the sleepwalker, has never strolled in his sleep since, but the effects of that day remain. I became a fastidious door locker. It's harder now that the kids are older because if I continue this, I will lock them out instead of in.

Does the terror ever go away? All I can say is that I can sleep only when I see three beds filled, and I hear three children breathing. Then I remember Gerald and remind myself that there are many like him in the world who will help me keep my children safe. I listen to his jazz CD and sleep for one more night.

If a Tree Falls in the Forest...

It was a beautiful fall afternoon, and Jacob and I could have been outside with Leah, enjoying the fresh, crisp air. But, the book, Harry Potter and *The Half-Blood Prince* by JK Rowling beckoned to us, and we were almost finished. We didn't even wait until bedtime. Instead, Jacob and I hunkered down on my bed after school to finish it off. We already knew the identity of the Half-Blood Prince, but we had not yet reached the part where a significant character dies. We were anxious to find out who was going to be the next victim of a forbidden curse in the sordid and engrossing tale of Harry Potter, who is referred to in the series as "the boy who lived."

Every once in a while, I would get up and look out my bedroom window and see Leah on the swing set. She was old enough at age seven to play outside in the backyard alone, but I felt better checking on her about every ten minutes or so. The backyard was not fenced in because it was connected to common land shared by the subdivision in which we lived.

Our property extended about twenty feet from the house, and the grass continued another twenty-five feet to a creek that ran behind the houses on our street. There were natural springs that kept water in the creek year round, but when it rained, it rushed with storm runoff. Often, we stood on the deck during a storm, watching the torrent, and wondering if it would flood onto the grass. We lovingly called this "dinner and show" (yes, we were desperate for a date night).

At first, being connected to this common land, where people walked up and down with their dogs or on a stroll, felt like others were walking through our yard. But the bonus for us was the extra space for the kids to play soccer, catch, football, and kickball, and explore the creek for frogs, tadpoles, and interesting rocks in the warm weather.

On the other side of the creek, a steep bluff goes straight up, covered in trees and brush. There were houses at the top of the hill we could see in the winter when the trees were bare. But in the summer, the foliage blocked them from view, and I fancied myself living in a national park.

Especially in the months when the trees were green, as I pulled into the driveway and entered the garage at the back of the house, I thanked God for blessing me with such a beautiful place to live—a place that provided my children with opportunities for play and adventure, and, at the same time, offered me beauty and serenity.

I had just popped up and, through my bedroom window, checked on Leah, who was swinging on the swing set. She seemed happy in her world for the moment— singing and swinging and content. I had not settled back for more than two minutes of the *Half-Blood Prince* when an ear-splitting crack came from the backyard. The entire staff of Hogwarts could have appeared in the room with a sound that startling. It was immediately followed by a crash that shook the ground and rattled the windows.

Jacob saw my terrified face and, before we could even start racing for the kitchen door, this child, who spends entirely too much time in my head, said, "She's all right, Mom."

We bolted for the kitchen, which led to the back door. Never in my life, in all the philosophical meanderings of trees falling, had I ever wondered, "If a tree falls in the forest, is my child dead?" All Leah had to do was decide to skip ten feet down to the creek to look at a rock, find a frog, or see if there were any tadpoles, and she would be in the path of dozens upon dozens of trees.

My heart pounded and my mind raced as I tried to force myself to remain calm until I had real information, none of which I had as I bolted from the bedroom. All I had was my nine-year-old son's reassurance ringing in my ears, "She's all right, Mom. She's all right." *How did he know the exact right thing to say?* I marvel at it to this day, sacred comfort coming from a child. It held me together for what felt like an eternity but, in reality, was probably ten seconds.

By the time we got to the back door, Leah was halfway up the stairs and almost on the deck herself. She was scared to death and shaken to the core. She ran as fast as she could toward the house—smart girl. Thank God she had stayed on the swing set and, for whatever reason, did not go to explore the creek that day.

As I feared, the tree had fallen right into our yard. There had been no gap between the sound of the crack and the thud shaking the ground—not even the space between seeing the lightning and hearing the thunder. We had felt it and heard it at the same time; it was in our backyard, not one house down or one house up from ours.

The tree, which was on the other side of the creek, had been rotting. It was hollow inside, and the recent heavy rains had weighed it down and rotted the bark that held it together until it finally gave way and just cracked. It stretched across the creek and into our backyard. The top branches were at most ten feet from where Leah had been swinging.

Jacob was correct. Leah was all right.

I, on the other hand . . . well, that's another matter. I still enjoy the beauty of where we live, but serenity is harder to come by. Perhaps if I had the wisdom and wizardry of the headmaster of Hogwarts, I might be able to rest easy. But, then again, he was the one who fell victim to a deadly and forbidden curse in *The Half-Blood Prince*, so maybe I am better off trusting God and the wisdom and strength of my children as witnessed in my own tale of "the girl who lived."

Kitchen Mesa

"I don't want anything bad to happen to him." Tears streamed down my face as I held our newborn, Daniel, in the rocking chair on his first day home from the hospital. At that moment I realized that a certain amount of terror would be my constant companion—terror about the vicissitudes and perils of life over which I had no control.

It may not be conscious all of the time, but this special brand of parental terror lives underneath the surface of things, like the pressure of a pimple forming underneath the skin when you can't see anything yet. It's a knot between my shoulder blades, the gurgling in the pit of my stomach, or the tension pulled across my temples.

It's difficult enough when one of my children experiences the pain that is a natural part of life—people being mean and nasty, failing at something for which they've worked hard, being really sick, or experiencing loneliness and anger. But it's worse when, through my own stupidity, stubbornness, or just plain human limitations, *I* am the cause of their distress or potential danger. I notice this happens when I am so close to being a good, effective parent; lest I get too full of myself, falling flat on my arrogant ass follows right behind.

One memorable occasion happened on our summer trip to Ghost Ranch. Leah was only four and a half, but we had already gone on a successful family hike into Box Canyon (see page 40), so Dan thought that our fierce little creature could handle the much bigger hike of Kitchen Mesa. The boys had already conquered this trek the year before at ages five and seven. I had never been on this hike, so I had to trust Dan's judgment.

After lunch, we rushed back to our casitas (one step above camping, with bunk beds in an adobe cube with communal bathrooms twenty yards away), filled our water bottles, snagged a few Gatorades, slathered on our sunscreen, and grabbed our hats. Our fearless hiking family was off on another great adventure as we made our way along the trail and through the brush behind the huge cliff-face towering above the dining hall (thus the name, Kitchen Mesa).

We were embarking on a four-hour hike over five miles that climbed from 6,500 feet above sea level to 7,100. It was a particularly hot afternoon, topping out at about ninety-seven degrees of dry, moisture-sucking heat. It didn't take long for the sun to become a merciless companion; I found myself missing the shady cover along the arroyo that led to Box Canyon.

Once behind the Estrada Cliffs, as they're officially called, we started our climb up the adjoining mesa that would lead us to the back of Kitchen Mesa and our goal— viewing the dining hall and the beautiful ranch from up above. Dan had told me that there was a narrow dirt path and then a rocky, fifteen-foot "chute" one had to climb through to get to the top of the mesa. I figured it must not be that bad if he thought Leah could do it. At least, that's what I thought before I saw it for myself. We stopped to rest and drink some water as we took in the next stage of our hike.

The narrow path was a thin, tilted strip of red dirt and loose gravel that stretched across a steep slope that looked fit for a trapeze artist, but not a preschooler, no matter how fierce. My stomach sank when I looked below the path and noticed a "catch wire" ten feet down and stretched across the gravel slope that you could grab if you slipped and headed down the rockslide.

What the f#@&% was he thinking?! I became so angry, I couldn't see straight. But I didn't want to ruin the family fun, so I remained silently incensed. He was confident all was well, and I couldn't believe what an idiot I had married. Plus, I was so hot and tired already, I wondered if I could make it through this hike. My pulse was already thumping, and it wasn't just because I was eating my anger. I felt physically worn out and couldn't quite figure out why.

I'm not that out of shape, I thought to myself. As my thoughts roiled in the blazing sun, Dan took the boys across the narrow path and came back for Leah's hand to guide her across. Loathe to be the "weak sister" who couldn't cut it on this family outing, I ignored my puzzling physical symptoms and picked my way across the narrow path while the kids and Dan started climbing hand over foot up the boulder-strewn trail toward the chimney-like chute in the corner.

Dan climbed with each boy through the chute and pushed Leah's little rump up the stone crevice where the boys were ready to grab her hands and help pull her up to the top. Dan came back down to boost me through, giving my rump a shove as well. I looked back down at the terrain we had just conquered and couldn't quite believe it. I was glad the hardest part was behind us (except for having to do it in reverse on the way back). It felt like we were almost there; little did I know we had at least another hour of walking, albeit on mostly level terrain, before we reached the front of the mesa and the view beckoning us forward.

By the time we made it to the front of the mesa, excitement overtook tiredness, and we rejoiced at meeting our goal. The kids inched a safe distance from the edge to catch a glimpse of the dining hall, and we took pictures in our victory stance. By this time, I was feeling completely spent and dehydrated, and my pulse was racing at a pretty good clip.

Dan looked at the water and Gatorade supply and realized we had one small bottle of Gatorade left to get the five us back down; we would have to ration it. I felt like I would need to guzzle about six of them just to get up to par. I didn't want to alarm the kids, but I had to let Dan know how awful I felt. It finally dawned on me that dehydration was one of the side effects of the migraine-prevention medicine I took. Hiking at high elevation in the blazing heat without enough fluids was a pretty bad idea.

Without too much delay, we headed back the way we came. The boys could tell I wasn't feeling well, so they took turns holding my hand when there was room for us to walk side by side. I had not anticipated how much strength I received from them to keep going; when we dropped hands to navigate a narrow portion of the trail, I could feel their energy drain out of my arm. I hung onto them as often as I could. When we shared a sip of the last Gatorade, everyone took one sip and I got two.

Worse than how I felt physically was the realization that I had put my whole family at risk for the sake of my ego. A new kind of terror gripped me. *What if the ration of fluids hadn't been enough for them? What if one of them got injured and Dan or I needed to hike out and get help?* I was a liability and in no shape whatsoever to help if something happened to one of our children or Dan.

Instead of a family hike with two parents and three kids, Dan was one parent with four kids; the only competent parent was the one I thought was an idiot just a short while ago. *Who's the idiot now?* The one who couldn't admit she was not feeling up for the whole hike when we were just an hour in.

Sliding down the chute and treading across the narrow path became harrowing on the way back, not because I was worried about my four-and-a-half-year-old, but because I was worried that my own body would give out. At some point, I knew that if I stopped moving, I would not be able to start again. When Dan and the kids took a break, I kept moving and drank my fluid rations while walking. Eventually, they would catch up to me.

The most painful moment of the trek came near the very end. They had stopped for their last break, and I was in front, getting close to the trailhead. Leah shouted from behind me, "Mommy, I want to be the first one to finish; I want to be first!" I heard her, but I couldn't respond. I just had to keep moving forward, and hoped I would be forgiven if it meant I didn't have to be carried out of the canyon on a stretcher. Thank God, my little Leah had more fierceness than even Dan knew. She ran full tilt, passed me by, and crossed the trailhead in front of me.

The next summer at Ghost Ranch, we got up at 5:00 a.m. and hiked Kitchen Mesa in the cool of the early morning before breakfast. I also took an art class called Retablo Painting. Started in Mexico, a Retablo depicts a watershed moment in the artist's life and includes a short paragraph written somewhere on the painting that describes how or why this event was life-changing. Believers used these paintings as a way to thank God for rescue, and the walls inside some Catholic churches were decorated with this touching folk art. I painted Kitchen Mesa for Dan, and on it I wrote:

What a blessing my children have a dad who will challenge them to risk within the safe bounds of his arms' reach. My mom has a framed cross-stitch piece that proclaims, "The kitchen is the heart of the home." But for me, "the Kitchen Mesa" is the heart of our home.

I'm not an artist, so it looks like a bad paint-by-number piece, but Dan says it's the best gift he's ever been given. Certainly he and the kids are mine.

The Terrible Awful

We didn't realize it at the time, but the chapter of our life I call "The Terrible Awful" began in 2007. In the late spring, Dan's uncle Henry died after a lifelong struggle with schizophrenia. We were so sad that our children had never had an opportunity to meet Uncle Henry, but he was a regular topic of conversation, especially when Jacob asked, "What if the way Uncle Henry's mind works is the right way and the rest of us are wrong?"

In September, Dan's mom had a stroke. Dan drove to Madison, Wisconsin, after work, arriving late into the night to see his mom. When he entered her room, Mel, one of the staff, was there sitting with her. His shift had ended more than two hours before, so Dan asked if he was working overtime.

"No," said Mel. "I knew you were on your way, and I didn't want her to be alone." Mel was one of many people who worked on the unit who were truly called and gifted in their ministry of caregiving for those with dementia.

Our kids wanted to join Dan in Madison so they would have a chance to say good-bye to their grandma. I was torn. I was worried that seeing her unconscious from the stroke would be traumatic for them, even though they had visited her in the Memory Care Unit several times. They were insistent, however, as insistent as any twelve, ten, and eight-year-old can be. I wasn't sure if it was the right thing to do, but we decided to go. The kids and I drove up to Madison and Gwen, the chaplain, met us as we stood around Grandma's bed.

Never have I been so glad that I had listened to my children instead of my own fears. Chaplain Gwen led the five of us in a *Blessing of the Body of One Who Draws Near to Death* by Joyce Rupp. We gave thanks for her ears, her eyes, her mouth, her hands, and feet—for the kindness they brought, the good they wrought, the joy they shared, and the love they offered. After each petition of gratitude, we said through tears, "You will always be in our hearts. Go in peace."

Joan lasted about ten days after her stroke; we got the call at home that she had passed away as we were eating cake for Jacob's eleventh birthday.

The next month, my favorite aunt became gravely ill, and I had just enough time to send her a letter of remembrance and gratitude, which my cousins read to her before she died.

Three weeks later, I found a lump in my right breast. I had an appointment with my ob/gyn the same week I found it. My doctor reviewed all the reasons I could have lumpy tissue in my breasts—caffeine, fibrous masses, and so on. Then he examined me and felt what I had found, and he had me stay in his office until he could get me an appointment with a breast surgeon. It wasn't looking good for the home team.

Within a month, I was diagnosed with two kinds of breast cancer (ductal and lobular) and had a double mastectomy. I was stage 2b and the cancer was not only in the lymph nodes, but invasive there as well. I had to have the right breast removed, but opted for both since the left one would have to be checked every six months by MRI to make sure the more aggressive of the two cancers had not spread. I decided I preferred to do surgery, chemotherapy, and radiation only once if at all possible.

My chemotherapy began the day after Christmas. I was told that some people had their treatment on Friday and went back to work on Monday. I did not know who these bionic people were, but that certainly wasn't my experience. I was plastered to the bed for at least a week following each treatment, and found it exhausting to hold a phone up to my ear while lying down. I had been the pastor at St. Mark's Lutheran Church for just a year when I was diagnosed and had to go on short-term disability during my treatment.

Dan was a solo pastor at Trinity, and we had three really busy children in seventh, fifth, and third grades. We would have never survived without a small army of help from both our congregations and other families who prepared meals, drove our kids to and from their sports practices and games, and put us on every prayer list imaginable. My breast surgeon assured us that I would not die from this cancer (although there were numerous times when it felt like I would), but it was impossible to experience cancer without confronting the reality of my own death.

How could I make peace with the possibility that I would not be there to finish raising my kids? To see them graduate from college, much less high school? To get married and have their own children? I could see this fear in

Dan's haunted eyes sometimes, yet the terror of losing me was not anything we could talk about then, when it felt too real.

I learned to mark small victories and take comfort in the passage of time. Another day passed meant I was one day closer to being done. I counted down the treatments and marked off how many days I would feel awful. I would delight in a day where I could fold a load of laundry or drive to the store to buy Easter candy. I trusted and hoped and fought and prayed to make it through.

In April, we got a call from Dan's sister in Madison, saying that their dad was having balance, memory, and other problems. My parents came up from Texas to take care of the kids and me, so Dan could go to Madison and take his dad for some tests. Dan was horrified to find himself on the cancer ward of another hospital with his dad. It was stage four brain cancer—a glioblastoma multiforme—the same diagnosis Ted Kennedy received a month later. It had been only seven months since Dan's mom died, and five months into my treatment. And now this. How was this possible?

The "Terrible Awful" became worse ten days later when we learned that our tax accountant had made an error in our estimated taxes and we owed $10,000 to the IRS. We were thankful that I had disability income, but that was only two-thirds of my regular salary, and we ended up with about $10,000 in medical bills, even with insurance. Now we were approaching $20,000 in the hole. We had to stop the kids' music lessons (trombone, cello, and violin) and were not able to sign them up for any summer camps.

Chemo or not, I couldn't get out of bed the next week. I read the book of Job and found the tenth chapter, called, "I Loathe My Life" to be a gripping expression of lament and anger toward God: "Does it seem good to you to oppress, to despise the work of your hands and favor the wicked? . . . Your hands fashioned and made me; and now you turn and destroy me . . . Let me alone, that I may find a little comfort before I go, never to return, to the land of gloom and deep darkness."

I now understood, in my bones, the powerful permission such words offer us when we are filled with anguish. God can handle the depths of human despair and would rather have us shout enraged than turn away in silence.

A month later, in May, I received a certified envelope in the mail. Inside was a Mother's Day card from my brother, Doug, which said, "I can't take chemo for you, I can't take radiation for you, but I can do this." Enclosed was a check for $7,000. I wept and wept. It was humbling to feel so loved, so supported, so important. Moreover, my two sisters, Pam and Julie, and two of my closest friends took vacation time from work to stay with us and help and shop and cook and clean and drive.

I had a break in treatment between the end of five months of chemotherapy and the start of six weeks of radiation. Our whole family drove to Madison to visit "Baba" (our kids' name for Grandpa). He and I took bald pictures together, and we tried to celebrate the completion of my chemotherapy.

As I slowly recovered and returned to work that fall, we hoped that the worst year of our lives was over and that we could breathe a little easier. Baba was still sick, but he was taking treatments that prolonged his presence with us, and we were so grateful for whatever time together we had.

That Christmas, however, my mom was hospitalized and diagnosed with advanced liver disease. She was really sick and needed consistent care and new daily habits to manage her body's diminished capacity.

By the fall of 2012, Baba had died, my mom had died, and her mom, my last grandparent, had died. My grandmother's death at age 101 was no surprise to any of us, of course, but by then, we were so exhausted from illness and death, we could hardly bear another loss. The "Terrible Awful" lasted just over five years.

It's taken quite a while for us to stop clutching against life and holding our breath as we waited for the next disaster or crisis. We released an unconscious sigh of relief two years after my grandma died because we made it that long without another health catastrophe or death in the family.

We realize that so many people have lives much harder than ours—not that such a reality diminishes the grief, pain, or anguish we have experienced—but it does help us keep our life and losses in perspective. We're not refugees fleeing war zones or other worse fates. We are blessed beyond measure because of the countless number of people who prayed, worked, listened, and supported us through the "Terrible Awful." We try to pay it forward whenever we can.

Revelation at the Food Court

ecently, I took Leah shopping for khaki pants, required dress for Character Choir at the elementary school. She started to get a bad headache and needed something to eat, so we went to the food court. It was about 4:00 p.m. If the world or even our household were run according to her clock, this would be dinnertime every day. She's not very hungry in the morning, but when she comes home from school, she's ready to pack it away. Give her a nice big serving of ice cream at 6:00 or 7:00 p.m., and that would be a perfect day.

Leah ordered the orange chicken—the kind you can get at any variety of Asian counters at the mall—with fried rice and a St. Louis specialty called crab rangoon. She was in heaven, eating just what she had imagined the day before, when we had planned our shopping trip.

I had a good-sized lunch and wasn't really hungry yet, but we were leaving for a church event and would miss dinner at home. I was unable to pass up a plate of food even though my body didn't need it at the moment.

I asked Leah how she was doing. It had been a hard run with Grandpa dying just a few months earlier after a long battle with brain cancer; I had gone through reconstructive surgery from breast cancer just before he died; and we still missed Grandma, who had died two years before from a stroke and the effects of Alzheimer's.

Was there anything Leah wanted to talk about? How was she feeling? It turns out she was worried about her other grandmother—Nana, my mom—who was battling liver disease. *How long will she live? Why is she sick?* Leah, like all of us, was bracing herself for the proverbial other (or, in our case, about the seventh) shoe to drop. So many bad things had happened, one right after the other. Who could possibly relax?

I tried to explain Nana's disease the best I could and reassure Leah that Nana was doing quite well. Morfar ("Grandpa" in Swedish) was healthy and doing a good job of looking after her. I looked down at this plate of food I didn't need, didn't want, and which didn't taste all that good. There was a pause in the conversation; I wondered why I was eating when I wasn't hungry.

The answer came to me like the fried rice sign flashing above the food court counter: I was racked with anxiety. I was trying to push the anxiety down and away with food. It didn't seem to be working. In fact, it made it worse because an unhealthy diet and weight gain caused even more anxiety about the recurrence of cancer. It was a vicious cycle.

Perhaps I just needed to ask myself the same questions I was asking Leah: *Is there anything I'd like to talk about? How am I feeling?* I knew one anxiety was the burden I felt at saddling my daughter with the increased risk of breast cancer, and my compulsion to keep her physically active and eating fresh fruits and vegetables. Another anxiety was wondering if I was leading a life of significant impact and meaning and working toward the goals I had set. It was my version of survivor guilt: *Was I living a life that is worth having survived cancer and deserving of all the people who helped us?*

As I let these and other anxieties bubble up into the fluorescent light of the food court, I saw that I have a lot of my own work to do. Once again, my children provided the context for me to see my true self more clearly.

I wonder how often it is true that the questions we ask others are the very ones we need to ask ourselves.

Matching Bras

Leah and I bought matching bras recently. We finally gave away our matching dresses I had bought when she was little. She wore her dresses from the time they hung at her ankles until they barely covered her little behind. I finally had to admit she was getting too big for our three-set parade of matching dresses.

But I could not just put them in bag on the front porch to go to the next charity that came by to pick up our donations. I could not take them to Goodwill. I couldn't bring myself to drop them in a clothing donation box at her school. It seemed silly to save them; I wouldn't wear my dresses without her counterparts, so why was I saving them? I don't make quilts or pillows or even patch jeans for that matter. No, the fabric would rot before the dress material would be put to good use.

I finally thought of a church member who was close enough to my size and who also had a little girl with room to grow. We put the matching dress sets together in a bag, brought them to church, and set them in the pew where the woman and her daughter normally sat, a gift of love and memories. We were so happy when our gift was accepted, and they came to church one Sunday clad in the red dresses, happily connected, the daughter not yet embarrassed by her mom.

Leah and I have not yet worn our matching bras. I don't know that they will offer that same sense of bonding and excitement at being alike that matching dresses did when Leah was four, five, and six. She was too embarrassed to join me in the store to buy new underwear, much less a real bra. I didn't even have real breasts, having just had reconstructive surgery three months before after a double mastectomy two years prior.

Developing breasts was not necessarily good news for my daughter and is accompanied by even more conflicted feelings for her than other girls. I couldn't quite fathom what it felt like for her to start growing what I've had cut off.

The blue satin waits in our drawers—a sacred offering of hope that eventually we can wear them with a smile and trust that whatever they cover is beautiful regardless of whether they're real or not—because they are matched with love.

~ 6 ~

FinDing GoD

God is a spirit that is both a boy and a girl—
like a seahorse or a worm!
—Daniel, age 7

Spirituality and Pregnancy

One of the most difficult things for me during pregnancy has been to let go of control over my body and my routine. Pregnancy requires me to allow the life that is within determine things I normally take for granted: what I can and cannot eat and drink, when and how much sleep I need, what kind of exercise I do, what kind of schedule I can keep, and so on.

From the moment I learned I was pregnant, the struggle to yield to the needs and the demands of this other life began. I find it odd that I am rearranging myself, my body, and my routine for a being I haven't even met yet! Now that I am approaching the end of this first pregnancy, I find myself thinking things like, "I'm ready to have my body back."

Yet, if I too anxiously reclaim the control I struggled to give up, I will miss the spiritual discipline that pregnancy provides. In 1 Corinthians 6:19, the Apostle Paul writes, ". . . your body is a temple of the Holy Spirit which you have from God . . . you are not your own." Pregnancy provides a disciplined pattern for paying attention to the life of God that dwells within us, for giving up the illusion of control and yielding to the demands and desires of the Spirit of God.

Deepening our relationship with God requires the same patient, acute attentiveness to the internal presence of the sacred—a life that, like an infant, brings wonderful blessings along with its demands; a life whose gifts we miss if we do not acknowledge and listen to it. Pregnancy offers up one way to live into God's claim on our life as we practice meditative attentiveness to that still small voice and the nudging of the Spirit of God.

I imagine that Mary, the mother of Jesus, was able to yield to God's will throughout her life and that of her son, because she first learned to yield to God in the womb.

Ranting and Raving

No one tells you that when you have children, you lose your own life. I think there's a conspiracy of silence among parents. No one tells you what it's really like to have kids and how it will change and affect you, your marriage, and your whole existence. Perhaps it's because we wouldn't believe it anyway, or we can't really know until we're in it.

Our life somehow seemed manageable with one child, but once Jacob was born, it all seemed to fall apart. Nothing worked any more. We had no time, no calm, no sanity . . . and way too much stress. The first week I went back to work after Jacob was born, it really hit us. Dan and I were both solo pastors of urban churches. Every night of the work week, one of us had a meeting, the boys were in two different daycares, and we had one Ford Escort wagon (we downsized to one car during my maternity leave to get out of debt). Even after we bought a minivan six weeks later, life didn't get a whole lot easier. Dan and I would look at each other as we got ready in the morning and say, "I love you; I hate our life."

I also cried as I dropped off the boys at daycare. This didn't trouble me so much when Daniel was a baby. He was going to a grandma-type who took care of three babies up to the age of one in her home. Part of me thought he was much better off spending the day with her than with me. I had this wonderful sense of freedom and gratitude. I was able to be a pastor and a mom. When I prayed about taking

Daniel to daycare as a baby, I had a wonderful vision of God being able to love him through other people, and that it was going to be okay. I felt peaceful about it.

But having a second child changed everything in ways I could not predict. My ob/gyn had told us, "One is like none, but two is like ten!" It made no sense to me until I actually had the two in my arms. With one, you have the illusion that your life is still your own, even just a little bit. The other parent can give the bath, and you can look at a magazine. The baby can go to sleep at seven or eight in the evening, and the two of you can watch a movie. There was a sense of trading off and having a little slice of time to oneself.

But with a two-year-old and a baby, you can kiss that slice of life good-bye. I was bathing one, and Dan was bathing the other. I was feeding one, and he was feeding the other. The diapers, the laundry, the dishes, the baby stuff didn't double but seemed to multiply exponentially. I had a hard time working and feeling I had enough one-on-one time with each of the boys when I got home, especially after evening meetings. I tried being the mom of an only child to Jacob, like I had been to Daniel, but that didn't work either.

So the crying and turmoil began. I couldn't spend enough time with them in the evening, so why was I leaving them during the day? Especially since the work at church was becoming increasingly stressful with such a small membership. Something had to give.

Dan was not crying as he dropped them off at daycare. Why was I bawling when he didn't even tear up? We didn't have an answer, so Dan would shrug his shoulders and say, "It's a mystery." We concluded that evolutionarily speaking, he is programmed to go kill the yak, so he drops off the babies and away he goes.

To my feminist sensibilities, it was hard to wrap myself around this new experience. I thought I would always work; I would be the Nike woman and "Just Do It" . . . and Just Do It all at once. Whether it was biology, sociology, evolution, socialization, psychology, personality, or some indeterminate combination, all I could conclude was that resigning from full-time ministry was the right decision for us as a family, and for me as a mother.

I would never claim it's the right decision for other women. If feminism gives us anything, I would hope it gives us the power of choice without fearing judgment from or by what someone else chooses. I have friends who are working mothers, and I'm glad their lives work for them. I don't think my choice is superior, simply because I cannot presume to know what constitutes the best choice for someone else. Mothers have worked for centuries, and many today do not have the financial opportunity to make a different choice, even though they may wish to.

The struggle for me is that I still had this feeling I had lost my life in a way that Dan had not. I didn't want to go back to the way it was, but, at the same time, I missed the freedom and independence of running my own day. It was an odd duality of conflicted experience: I had made a choice; yet, it felt like a sacrifice when Dan did not make a comparable one.

The other day, I was exhausted and stressed from being home with kids, craving silence and time alone. The kids went to the basement to play, and I stood in the middle of the house and cried, "I had a life once. What happened to my life? I just want my life back!" Only the furniture and the walls heard me. They gave no response. But, somehow, saying it out loud helped me feel that I still was a person.

These were the moments that helped me understand the Book of Psalms. I felt bad about being so frustrated and lost sometimes, always being the caretaker and not quite ever feeling cared for myself. That was the craziness of being home with small children. Then I tried to remind myself that I stood in a tradition of holy ranting and raving: "How long must I bear pain in my soul?" (Psalm 13:2) "My God, my God, why have you forsaken me?!" (Psalm 22:1)

The psalmists' pain might be different from mine, but the need to rant and rave once in a while is still the same. The relief comes, not in receiving an answer, but in the crying out itself, because to do so is to trust that God is paying attention, and that I am not alone.

Cry Room

It seems that most Sundays when I attend worship, I feel like crying. Sundays are just hard in general. Sitting in the pew instead of being up front. Watching my husband lead worship and preach. Seeing the awe and admiration on the faces of his parishioners. Wondering why God wants him up there, but not me. Feeling relieved that I don't have to be up there because it's just too stressful to do all that and take care of three small children. Yet, feeling resentful at the same time that he gets to do his work and I don't. That having children has radically changed my life, but not his. It's an inner-conflict-o-rama, as if a taffy-machine has commandeered my soul.

I miss the liturgy of Lutheran worship, and I really miss weekly Holy Communion. And I feel forgotten, as if I'm invisible on God's radarscope and have fallen off the map since I am no longer serving a congregation.

There's something about staying home with little kids that can make one feel like a non-person. Children are so needy and demanding and relentless, there doesn't seem to be any room for me or my needs. I don't always feel this way, of course, but I have moments every week when I think I'm going insane.

The health and well-being of our children is the most important priority in our lives, and I don't question that. I just wonder why it's so hard for me to yield myself to this new role, a role I chose. No one held a gun to my head and said, "Have three children, exactly two years apart!" But when I started at age thirty-two, I wasn't going to sit around and wait to age myself into a higher-risk category.

I take this jumble of confused thoughts and feelings and attend worship at my husband's church. I sing and hear and say words like, *"His eye is on the sparrow, and I know he watches me . . . O Lord my God, I cried to you for help, and you have healed me . . . Beyond the sacred page I seek Thee, Lord; my spirit pants for Thee, O Living Word! . . . We trust in Jesus . . . Jesus proclaimed the reign of God . . . blessing the children, healing the sick, and binding up the brokenhearted . . ."* And I am moved to tears. Almost every week. It's profoundly moving to affirm one's faith in the midst of the confusion and pain of daily life and feel as though you've moved back into God's view, and all of my inner conflict has not chased God away.

But who wants to be exposed and bawling in the middle of a stiff, proper Anglo-Saxon worship service? Not anyone. Not me. Certainly not the pastor's wife. We are the frozen chosen. Sometimes, I wonder if I should worship in an African-American congregation where the free expression of feelings as to how the Spirit has touched you is not only accepted, but also expected. But such free expression is neither expected nor as easily accepted in our traditions (that's also true of Lutherans and most Protestants, for that matter). So, there I sit, feeling claimed by God once again, but holding it in, trying to ignore how I feel so I can fight back the tears. Pretend you have a cold or something in your eye. *Get yourself under control,* I tell myself.

The sermon was on healing. I couldn't tell Dan what I thought of it, because I didn't listen to it. I couldn't. It was too close. I had to think of something else, like when I last plucked my eyebrows, the best way to burn the *Barney* videos, why I found a can of corn in the back of the basement toilet—anything except God's healing, anything besides how much God loves me, mess that I am. So, worship was actually doing exactly what I needed, but I had to push away the experience and try to revisit it later when I was alone.

I suddenly wished there was a cry room for adults. The first parish I served had one for children. It had a glass window to see the worship service, a speaker to hear it, chairs for adults, and toys for children. Parents could enjoy the service, while being with their children, but sparing everyone else the disturbance they might cause.

Why not have a cry room for grownups who need and want to be in worship, but who are in pain? We could participate in worship but not be exposed. We could receive what we need without disturbing anyone else. It could be stocked with tissues, a table with the pastor's business card, a mirror on the wall so you could get yourself together before going out for fellowship, and a retired pastor who could put an arm around you and tell you that everything is going to be okay.

Of course, there's something offensive about the idea, just like there is about a cry room for kids; we should somehow be able to welcome all people as they are in worship and make it accessible for everyone. We should be comfortable enough within ourselves to be who we are regardless of what others think. There may be congregations where this actually happens, but in mainline Protestant church culture, I don't think it will become the modus operandi any time soon.

Today, I would rather have a cry room and not feel like I have to push away the very experience of God I need.

Angel's Wings

I received a phone call from Scott's mom, Virginia. Scott was a young man who died of AIDS when I was a pastor in Kansas City. Scott had lived in the neighborhood of the congregation I served, and I had visited him in the last stages of his illness and presided at his funeral. Scott was lovingly cared for in his illness and death by his partner, Jim. Over the years, Virginia has kept in touch with me and even crocheted a beautiful blanket for Jacob when he was born.

On this day in September, Virginia was calling about Jim. Jim had been trying unsuccessfully to get in touch with me for several months. Because we had moved twice since I left that congregation, he was having a hard time tracking me down and finally called Scott's mom to help him. Jim was dying of brain cancer and wanted to talk with me before he died. Virginia wondered if I could give him a call and gave me his phone number.

Jim was still very young, maybe in his late thirties or early forties. Brain cancer. It just didn't seem fair. He had lived a hard life already, and this just seemed cruel. But it was even worse than I thought. I called him, and we talked, cried, and prayed on three different occasions before I called and heard the phone ring and ring and ring, with no one there to answer.

In the years since I had seen Jim, his brother and his father had both died. His mother lived nearby but didn't come to see him very often—maybe once a week, which isn't very often in my book when your child is dying. Jim and I talked about it, thinking perhaps she just couldn't take the pain after losing her husband and a son already. Amazingly, in his pain, Jim had compassion for her.

Hospice workers came to visit and help care for him. But the real saving grace was that he had a new partner, Gary, who was retired and able to care for him with the same love and patience with which Jim had cared for Scott.

Like many terminally ill people, Jim had few visitors. The discomfort of illness, the awkwardness of not knowing what to say, and the confrontation with one's own mortality keeps people at a distance. This was particularly true for a gay man in a small town in Missouri whose mother could only manage a visit once every week or two.

Jim was lonely, but not lost; forgotten, but not forsaken; down, but not in despair. That was why he wanted to talk to me before he died. "I wanted to thank you for giving me my faith in Christ. You didn't have to treat Scott and me the way you did. We weren't members. You didn't have to welcome us. But you did. My relationship with Christ is what has kept me going through all this, and it's because of you that I have that. I just needed you to know that and thank you for it."

I could hardly speak. Cry, maybe—a lot, actually—but not speak. How blessed I was to serve a congregation like St. Mark's, which had committed itself (long before I arrived) to intentionally welcoming gay and lesbian people and loving everyone, no exceptions. While Scott could still stand, I performed an informal, intimate commitment service for them with just two of their family members present, including Virginia. It was important to them to acknowledge their commitment and life together before Scott died.

It wasn't a "marriage" per se, but rather an acknowledgment of them as whole people, an integration of the life they shared, and an acknowledgement that God's embrace was big enough to include them. What peace it gave to Virginia, especially after Scott died. What peace it gave to Jim, who was able to truly live the rest of his life and withstood a very painful death, trusting in God's love for him.

This commitment service was against our denominational policy at the time; I spoke with my bishop about it and fortunately, he did not bring me under church discipline for what I believed to be a crucial part of pastoral ministry. Since then, we and other denominations have moved toward full inclusion of LGBTQ (Lesbian, Gay, Bisexual, Transgendered, Queer) people. For all of Christianity's attempts at judgment and exclusion, I have yet to see where that attitude has saved one soul. Scott's family carried a profound faith, and Jim not only believed, but also shared his faith, leading others to believe.

When Jim no longer answered the phone, I continued to call periodically until I finally caught Gary. He told me that Jim had died peacefully in his sleep one night. Gary was also comforted knowing how much Jim's faith meant to him and how much he talked about it. And the circle of faith continues to expand.

Who knows how many came to faith because of Jim? I can't answer that, but I do know that two angels in heaven named Scott and Jim have their wings all because one small, struggling, urban congregation shouted a resounding "YES!" when most others said, "No."

Earth is Crammed with Heaven

One day last fall, I was followed by butterflies—two monarchs, to be exact. They flew by the back sliding door off the kitchen at breakfast. One landed on the deck just on the other side of the glass and slowly lifted its wings up and down as if to communicate a message to me. About an hour later, I was in the front of the house, in the living room, and two monarch butterflies flew across the picture window, just inches from the glass so I could not miss them.

People who know our house may not think this is all that remarkable. We have a "butterfly bush" in our backyard with big purple flowers that attract butterflies of all kinds. But I thought it a bit unusual that this pair seemed to be appearing outside the window at the exact moment I was there, rather than resting on the bush in back, sucking up the nectar of the flowers.

I have come to believe that these gifts of nature are signs of God's presence, inviting me to be mindful of the goodness that surrounds me. Others might insist that the butterflies in the back and front of my house have nothing to do with God, that they are simply a function of fortuitous landscaping.

That afternoon, I went to an office supply store a couple miles from my house. It's on a busy street with two lanes of traffic going in each direction and a turn lane in the middle. There are no trees or butterfly bushes to speak of—

just stores, car dealerships, restaurants, and other businesses. I parked the car in the lot and stepped out. As I did, two monarch butterflies flew right past me. Whether intended or not, this trilogy of monarch pairs was comforting to me. I received them as a sign of God's providence in my life. New life would be forthcoming in some way.

If these delicate creatures can fulfill their lifespans through three distinct phases—caterpillar, pupa, and butterfly—then surely I can fulfill a larger purpose.

This gift of hope came not as some great act or grand gesture, but just by noticing, just by paying attention to butterflies. I have begun to notice birds more, as well. We have a creek that runs behind our house and is surrounded by quite a few trees, so there are plenty of reasons for nature to abound here. Other people have hanging plants, bird feeders, and such on their decks—things that encourage nature to come knocking on their back doors. I have none of these.

I do well to get my family bathed and fed every day, so the day I found out I was pregnant with our third child, all the houseplants were given away. I could be responsible for three other living creatures and a husband, but that was my limit. No plants, no pets. Even so, the signs of the Spirit's presence and comfort come to me. There is no food for them, but birds fly right up on our deck, sit on the grill, and look at me sitting at the kitchen table.

One day, Dan and I were sitting on the living room couch for a rare moment of quiet conversation—rare in the sense that we have three kids playing on five sports teams with the attendant practices, games, and parent concession-stand duties this season—and a sparrow flew near, sat on the narrow brick ledge outside the window, and sang a beautiful song. Perhaps it was a love song for his heartthrob across the street, but I received his tune as a love song for us, as well. Truthfully, I had no idea how well sparrows could sing.

Another day, I was driving back from a doctor's appointment and was upset for a reason I can no longer remember. I pulled over to the side of the road for a good cry and, when I looked up, a bird was perched on the parking sign right in front of me. While I watched, it flew behind the van and perched on a branch as if to say, "The Spirit goes before you and behind you, and you will be okay." I dried my eyes, said a prayer of thanksgiving, and went on my way.

Since a dove flew out of the Ark and returned with an olive branch for Noah, then why isn't every bird I see a sign of God's presence? If the Holy Spirit came upon Jesus in the form of a dove, then isn't every bird a small sign of the Spirit? If His eye is on the sparrow, perhaps God sends the sparrow to comfort me. That may sound arrogant, myopic, or self-centered. Perhaps none of these creatures are sent specifically for me. But it seems to me that we can look at nature and see just a bird, or we can see a bit of God.

Elizabeth Barrett Browning said it best in her poem, from which this essay derives its name:

> *Earth's crammed with heaven,*
> *And every common bush afire with God;*
> *But only he who sees, takes off his shoes,*
> *The rest sit round it and pluck blackberries.*

Barrett Browning and St. Francis of Assisi, who wrote the words to the hymn, "All Creatures of Our God and King," beckon us to pay attention to the miracles of nature and God's presence in it, which surround us every day. I discussed this view of miracles and the choice to see a bird or holy ground with my son, Jacob, one night when I was tucking him into bed. He is the middle child who struggles most verbally with faith and a belief in God. I sat down beside my eight-year-old's bed and said that it was time for prayers. The verbal volleyball began.

"Prayers don't do any good. Why does God get to be this great Spirit-thing, and I don't? And how come there aren't any miracles today like in the Bible?"

It may just be a form of procrastination, but it's a pretty sophisticated form, if you ask me. I hated to shut down the questions just because it was bedtime, and I was exhausted. So we talked a little bit about it. I told him there are lots of miracles today. I know people who have been healed of diseases and other problems through prayer and faith. Maybe he just hadn't met anyone like that yet. I explained that some miracles are small; we just have to keep our eyes open and look for them. Sometimes, we don't see them because we are not paying attention.

I told him that someone, though I don't remember who, told me a story about a woman whose mother loved ladybugs and, after the mother died, this woman would see ladybugs in the strangest places. She knew the ladybugs were sent by her mother and God to let her know everything was okay and that she would be all right. Once, in the winter when it was cold and snowy, the woman saw a ladybug on the porch railing. It was like a miracle—this red ladybug in the freezing snow.

Jacob seemed to find this intriguing, so I went on. I reminded him that our close friend, pastor, and spiritual mentor, "Uncle Sam," had something similar happen to him. His best friend died, and Sam was so sad. He told us that, one day, he was walking through a wooded area, and he walked under a tree full of golden leaves. A gust of wind came up just at that moment, and all the leaves on the tree let go at once and showered down upon him like a delicate blanket. He knew it was his best friend and God sending him comfort and love.

Jacob pondered these stories. He asked, "When you die before me, will you communicate with me if you're still alive, somehow?"

"Yes, I will, Jacob. If there is a way to communicate with you, I will do it. But you have to promise me one thing."

"What's that?" he asked.

"You have to promise that you will pay attention—pay attention and watch for the miracles."

Jacob thought this was a fair deal; he promised to pay attention. Then he said, "I was killing bugs this afternoon. I'll have to stop doing that in case you come back as one."

Resolve

The other morning I was walking into the living room, tea in hand, to sit in my prayer chair (an Amish bentwood rocker by the window). It was after breakfast, the boys were already on the bus, and Leah hadn't made an appearance yet. Our dog, Marcie, (who we rescued for the children's birthdays) was lying near the window with her head under my rocker. As I stepped into the room, she threw up her entire breakfast and medication right where I was headed for my morning prayers. *Lovely.*

I cleaned it up and soaked the spot with Resolve pet stain cleaner. I sat down to do my devotions while the Resolve beneath me worked its magic. The irony was not lost on me. While the cleaner was lifting the stains on the carpet, I was praying for my own stains to be removed. Some days, devotions are murky and the messages unclear; but this day, it was a little too plain.

When I manage to take time for morning prayers, my issues, concerns, anxieties, and sins are resolved more peacefully and lifted more easily. I've often said that the Spirit needs to hit me in the head with a two-by-four to get a message through my intractable stubbornness.

I really hate barf. Maybe I could keep my eyes open for messages with a little more subtlety.

~ 7 ~

Letting Go

*Leah, what did you do with the rose
petals that fell off the flowers?
I threw them outside so they'll fly away
with mercy and joy on the wind.*
—Leah, age 5

Surrender

I thought we were going to stop at two kids. I wanted to have them before I turned thirty-five when the risks increase, and I did. Daniel was born when I was thirty-two and Jacob when I was thirty-four. But just as we approached their third and first birthdays, I began thinking about another child, almost to the point that it was all I could think about. When I closed my eyes and pictured my family, there was always a baby in my arms. I felt like I was missing a person, like there was supposed to be someone else in our family who was not yet here.

I stared at families with more than two kids, to the point of rudeness. I would try to figure out how we would get a table in a restaurant, fit in a car, pay for college—heck, pay for preschool—but none of these questions seemed to matter. I closed my eyes and pictured my family; there was that baby again.

When I first brought it up to Dan, he brushed me off. By about the third time, he decided he really needed to listen to me. When he did and I explained what I had been going through and my gut feeling that someone was missing, he just said, "Ahhhhh. I guess we're having a third child." He would have been fine stopping at two, but he could tell that this desire was coming from deep within and beyond me. He immediately and intuitively knew it was going to happen, so he didn't protest or try to reason me out of it.

I was working pretty hard at that myself—trying to reason myself out of it—but it didn't work. We were missing a person, and I would feel incomplete, unsettled, and restless until this person who would complete our family arrived. We conceived after our second month of trying (always disappointing to Dan, who would like to have "tried" longer!). My due date was mid-October, just three weeks after Daniel would turn four and Jacob, two.

I got a phone call two days ago from my ob/gyn. She's never called me at home except when we paged her at the beginning of my previous two labors. I knew it couldn't be good news. It wasn't. My blood test that screened for Down's syndrome had come back with a positive indication that the baby could be affected. We needed to decide whether or not we wanted to go ahead with amniocentesis to find out for sure.

Though we decided to have the test, we couldn't imagine aborting for this reason. Still, it would be hard to wait for five months to find out. And, if it did turn out to be a Down's baby, it would give us time to prepare and learn more. Of course, there was a real chance it might not be Down's. My doctor said that, in her practice, over half of the cases like this do not turn out to be Down's.

I did little else but cry since I received this news. I wasn't sure why I kept crying and why it was so hard to stop. It was not what we imagined or hoped for our third child, so part of it was the loss of innocence and hope about having a healthy child. We wanted what was best for our child. Life was hard enough when you're mentally and physically healthy, and like most parents we knew, we didn't want our child to suffer. Our life and my career would certainly be changed drastically by a special-needs child, so that was part of it, too. I judged myself for crying so many tears, though. I didn't believe quality of life was determined by our physical nature. Wholeness and happiness came from the spirit, the soul of a person.

I was reminded of the sermon based on Colossians 3:14 my father-in-law preached at our wedding, "Above all, clothe yourselves with love, which binds everything together in perfect harmony." I remembered his message that "perfect harmony" was not the same as our worldly understanding of perfection. We were not seeking perfect harmony in terms of being flawless, but rather of coming to "complete maturity" together; growing into the fullness of who you are and your potential.

I did not feel adequate to be a mother of a special-needs child. I was afraid I wouldn't be good enough, patient enough, loving enough, self-sacrificing enough. Did God really have that much confidence in me? In my husband? In our marriage? In our family? Could we be the family that helped this person come to his or her full potential even as he or she helped us become our true selves?

Ultimately, the tears were about surrender. Surrender to that which was beyond my control. Surrender to God's will. Surrender to accepting, loving, and rejoicing in this person who was growing inside of me. Surrender to waiting. The test wasn't for five more days, and it would take two to three weeks to get the results. Finally, I had surrender and trust that no matter what happened, I would not be alone.

We felt better just going in for the test. We spoke with a geneticist first, who clarified the odds of Down's were one in 178. After that first phone call, it felt more like fifty-fifty. The doctor finally called with results. She said, "You're having a perfect little miss," meaning it was a girl who did not have Down's syndrome.

We did not find out the sex of the boys before they were born, but I felt so out of control in this situation, I wanted every piece of information they could give me.

It was a relief, I will admit. But it was also good to reflect again on helping to bring one another to perfect harmony as a family, whoever each of these children turn out to be. And that surrendering to what we can't control would always be part of the process.

The Stuff that Tells Our Stories

We drove from St. Louis to Madison, Wisconsin, to visit Dan's parents over Memorial Day weekend. We would see his dad at their house and his mom, Joan, in the Memory Care Unit where Dan had helped his dad move her that spring. This was the first time the kids and I would see Joan since she had been moved to this unit.

Joan loved cats, so the kids and I went to Build-A-Bear and made a stuffed cat for her to hold and keep on her bed. The kids each put a satin heart in the cat before it was sewn up, so they could feel that their love would remain with Grandma after we drove back home.

The Memory Care Unit was a beautiful, well-run place that looked and felt more like a home than a nursing facility. Each wing comprised a contained community with a kitchen where the residents ate around tables, making it feel homey, rather than like an institution. There was a big fish tank, along with a cockatoo named Sundance. Cats roamed the halls; a small aviary with unusually colorful birds hugged the wall that connected the hallways of residents' bedrooms. Activity and TV spaces were decorated like living rooms. Stacks of straw hats with colorful ties sat like a pillar next to the courtyard door, ready for anyone who wanted to take a sunny stroll outside. Art and wallpaper adorned the walls, and, blessedly, the whole atmosphere lacked the sickly urine smell that imposed itself in many such places.

The most striking feature of this center was outside of the patient rooms. Next to each door was an enclosed window with shelves that held items belonging to the person who lived in that room. Their names were there as well, of course, but these were all dementia patients. The progression may change, but for Joan as others, this illness resulted in the loss of language, then memory and physical tasks, and, finally, body functions as brain cells die. Dementias like Alzheimer's are eventually fatal and we were losing her brick by brick.

While Joan may not have been able to read her name on the wall, she did recognize her belongings in the window next to her door, which helped her to know which door was hers. Inside the window sat a pair of porcelain quails, some pieces of her china, a mug with a picture of one of her daughter's on it, three carved bears, and several other pictures of family members. These were just a few items, but they marked significant points in Joan's life.

The items told her story, that she belonged, and that her story was ongoing, whether she could remember all of it or not. The picture on a mug was of her daughter, Cynthia, who died of a congenital heart defect at age thirty-five. It was a reminder that life is precious and fragile, as Cynthia's was, and needed to be held carefully with love. Her death broke Joan's heart, and she treasured having many pictures of Cynthia nearby.

The teacup and creamer were from her mother's Spode China. Its white background with an intricate purple flower design represented elegance and beauty, hospitality, and cooking, holidays, and celebration. The two ceramic quails were on her mother's dining room table for as long as Joan could remember and then were passed on to her. They represented her childhood, continuity, love passed down from generation to generation, her hometown of Butler, Pennsylvania, and belonging.

There was a picture of Joan as a teenager, so full of hope and expectation, most of which was fulfilled in a wonderfully generous life. On the bottom shelf were three carved wooden bears that her husband, Dan, had made. Two were salt and pepper shakers, and the third was a sugar bowl. They spoke of love and homemade grace, of deeper meaning in simplicity and family, of bread and wine, of sacrament and community.

Joan was an only child, and she wanted a big family. She had five children and seven grandchildren. Three of her grandchildren peered out of the window at her from a picture taken at Easter. Finally, the picture of Joan and her husband told the story of fifty-three years of marriage to the man who came daily to visit, reminding her that her life was still marked by love and that she still belonged to him and to God.

Walking down the hall of doorways, one literally had a window into the lives of every person who lived here. The residents may not have been able to tell their own stories, but their treasures told part of it. One woman collected turtles, and her window was full of them. Another man was a war veteran. Those with large families filled their windows with photographs to keep them connected to people in their stories. Dementia or not, when they saw their things in the windows, they knew which door represented home.

This experience gave new meaning to our attachment to stuff. It helped to tell our stories when we couldn't, when words weren't enough, when we needed something more. The same seemed to be true in congregations, where people could be terribly attached to possessions.

Throughout history, many have been obsessed with the relics of the faith—the holy grail, the Ark of the Covenant, the actual site where Noah's ark was supposed to have landed, the Shroud of Turin, bits of the cross on which Jesus was crucified.

Several cathedrals in Europe, which I have visited, claimed to have a piece of the cross. I always thought it was rather silly. But as I thought back on those little bits of wood encased in glass, I realized people clung to them to help them tell part of their story as Christians. Having these pieces not only provided evidence or "proof" of our faith, but helped tell the story of Jesus' life, death, and resurrection. The meaning of his story became ours.

During my pastoral internship, I went to a nursing home to do a round of visits. The nurse was trying to feed a very obstinate, agitated old man who was a former surgeon and no longer in his right mind.

She looked at me helplessly when I walked in and said, "You might as well visit; I'm not getting anywhere with him."

Still being in seminary, I really had no idea what I was doing. I just thought something familiar would help him. I read Psalm 23, the most familiar thing I could think of, and held his hand. He cried and cried. I said the Lord's Prayer, told him it was all right, and that God loved him. I wiped his eyes.

The nurse came back in and fed him lunch, and he was a perfect pussycat. She looked at me like I was a miracle worker; but of course, it wasn't I who performed a miracle. It was the Word; it was experiencing the stuff of home and the things that were most familiar that connected him to his identity. He just needed to be reminded of his story and that even though he could no longer save lives and was being fed like a baby, he still belonged and lived in a spiritual home that would care for him now and forever. So much was gone, but like the stuffed cat with three hearts, he needed to know that love remains. Isn't that what all of us really need?

We live in a post-modern era where Christianity and mainline denominations are relegated to the margins of society. Our impulse is to try to save our structures and institutions, to look inward rather than outward. I wonder if this new era will drive Christianity in America far enough to the edge for us to distinguish the essential stuff from the non-essential stuff.

What would happen if we were willing to make a window next to our church door, with only the essentials we need to remember our identities, share our stories, and connect us to our mission of love? The world may not begin to beat a path to our door, but we might at least begin to recover from our dementia, and know that we are home.

Mini-van, Mini-me

My van recently died. Really died. It had over 164,000 miles on it, and it blew a head gasket in the parking lot of the elementary school that Jacob and Leah attend. It was Maundy Thursday, three days before Easter, but there was no resurrection for this dear old car. The mechanic called the day after Easter to confirm the feared diagnosis.

"It's time to lay it to rest," he said. "You would have to put in a new engine, and with the mileage on it, that doesn't make a whole lot of sense."

"It's time to lay it to rest." The words rang in my ears as I called my husband to relay the news. He was not surprised and showed no emotion. He was, in fact, somewhat relieved to be free of this cumbersome hunk of metal that had required two transmissions, a head gasket, several brake jobs, numerous tires, more recall repairs than one could count and never drove straight after I was rear-ended at a stoplight by a woman who fell asleep driving home from the night shift.

I, however, was crushed beyond belief. I felt as if my dog had died. Someone who had been with the family for years was gone, and I could barely tell Dan what the mechanic said without choking up. My husband found this humorous in a loving sort of way. After fifteen-and-a-half years of marriage, he was accustomed to living with "a crier." Dan had seen me choke up at Special Olympics commercials, weep through countless movies, sappy or not, and tear up during any conversation having to do with human fulfillment. He would not be surprised if I cried at a grocery store opening, so why not when my van died?

At first, I thought that my sadness was because my children had been raised in this van. We bought it when Jacob was four months old, Daniel was two years, and Leah was a twinkle in our eyes. It drove them to daycare, Parent's Day Out, and preschool. It met them at the bus when they started elementary school. It also took us many places as a family: to the zoo and the botanical garden and on vacation. We drove it to New Jersey, California, New Mexico, Texas, Minnesota, and states in between.

In that van, we listened to books on tape, watched our first videos in a bag that hung between the seats, and sang to the Beatles and the music of our good friend, Steve Eulberg. I started my business in this van, drove to appointments, stored products, and made deliveries.

I took comfort in knowing we had bought the van with the highest safety rating at the time. I entrusted my babies to this two-ton mound of metal and took the leap of faith we all do when we get behind the wheel.

Perhaps I was attached not just because of the memories it held and that it was the vehicle in which my kids grew up. Maybe the van carried symbolic significance for me. Cars are very important identifiers in our culture, connected to identity, self-perception, income level, image, and social status. I have always considered myself above such mundane considerations. I thought I didn't need society's traditional status symbols as the source of my identity and self-image. How rude an awakening self-awareness could be.

I had been a professional with a full-time career when I bought the van, but five months later, I became a stay-at-home mom. One year after I bought it, I started a home business. Now that the van was dead, I had to decide if I wanted to continue with the home business or go back to being a pastor. I'd lost my symbolic identity, and I'd have to figure out who I wanted to be without my van informing society who I was.

I think the van was also a symbol of my independence. Having moved every four years as I was growing up, I never had the luxury of being rigidly attached to forms of worship, houses, places, or even people. I knew they would change. Nonetheless, it created the illusion that I was not attached to anything in particular. I am not a collector of stuff. I prefer to collect ideas, experiences, and relationships. Perhaps this was why my attachment to a "thing" had caught me by surprise.

In fact, because I had subconsciously looked for identity and symbolic meaning in the van, I could see now that maybe this had held me back from achieving greater success in my Mary Kay business. When I won my first car, I "let" Dan drive it because, if I drove it, I would have had to give up the van and the safety, security, and story of myself that went with it. When I won the second car, we took the cash compensation instead of the vehicle. I had come so close to winning the next car up the career path two or three times but never quite got there. I think I may have been sabotaging myself because I hadn't wanted the car.

Clearly, I wouldn't let go of the van until it gave up the ghost, it was pried from my fingers, and there was no other choice. I couldn't choose to give it up. It had to die or be taken from me.

We were donating the van to the Salvation Army, which would either repair it or sell it to someone who would use it for parts. We received a tax deduction for the donation. We went to the mechanic yesterday to clean it out and to allow me to say goodbye.

As we drove up, I couldn't find the van at first. Then, I saw it behind a chain link fence off to the right, where the broken cars were. It was so sad. We cleaned it out, and Dan brought the keys back to the office and gave me a moment to say goodbye. I sat in the driver's seat and cried like a baby, still confused about why I was so sad. I have a better idea today, but, more important, I realized it's time to let it go and move on.

The new van arrived five weeks later. Dan drove it back from New York to St. Louis. We had purchased it sight unseen from a clergy couple who are the daughter and son-in-law of Dan's parishioners. The couple had moved to Manhattan and no longer needed it. It had been checked out by a mechanic there; the price was right; and, coincidently, Dan was flying to New York for a board meeting at just the right time. This couple always bought red cars because they had heard that people with bright-colored cars had fewer accidents because people noticed them.

Well, I took one look at the new van and thought people in the next county would be able to see it! It was fire-engine red—not burgundy, not maroon, not pomegranate—but aggressive, bright RED. I certainly wouldn't have a hard time finding that in a parking lot.

I hoped I wouldn't have as hard of a time finding myself either. Embracing the new wheels meant accepting that my children were getting older and the "little kid" stage of life was behind us. I was still in the driver's seat, but that would change, too. I prayed for the grace to enjoy the present time and let go of what was past, so I could embrace the adventures on the next leg of the journey.

Enjoy the Ride

J acob, our middle child, always has his creative juices flowing. Last week, Dan was out of town, and I tried to get this distractible kid to finish his homework. He procrastinated in many and various ways, all of which had me cracking up, making it harder and harder to be the enforcer of disciplined evening activity.

On this particular night, Jacob put on a cowboy hat and fake moustache and made faces in the mirror as if he were posing for a celebrity photograph. Then he went to talk with Leah. He came out of her room wearing her pink bra with the straight-faced statement, "I am a 34A."

Dan recently bought him new boxer briefs for his martial-arts class. Jacob used all that firm space in the bottom of the crotch to carry around his Gameboy, walking like he had a loaded diaper, and then showed me how accessible the game is through the boxer's "front door." (These antics seem to have a theme . . .)

Another evening, he came into the living room announcing that he could play three kazoos at once—one through his mouth and one through each nostril—and play he did.

He went to a co-ed camp for a week this past summer, during which they stayed out in the woods. One of the young girls offered a new tampon, in the absence of newspaper, to get the fire started. Jacob grabbed the cylindrical tube at the bottom of the applicator and tried to blow it like a whistle. No one thought it would work. They didn't know Jacob very well; he blew out tune after tune. When he didn't want to do homework, the little lavender tube came out and he played his "tamponica." Dan and I wondered if we're raising the next Jack Black.

If we needed a good laugh, we looked at the pictures from our trip to Disney World where Jacob made a weird face in every pose with the characters around the park, or we told each other Jacob stories and had instant comic relief from the stresses of daily life.

Who said parenting isn't fun? Somehow, the homework got done, especially when I had the patience to let go and enjoy the ride.

Letting Go

This week, Daniel turned sixteen and earned his driver's license. I have known this was coming; we even bought a third car so he could help us with errands in addition to driving himself to school. Because we planned for this and in many ways looked forward to it, I did not think I would be upset by this life transition. Not surprisingly, I was wrong.

I was usually out of sorts in September before all three of our children had their birthdays. A new school year had begun, they were moving forward in their lives, and time has brought us to this moment before I was ready or felt old enough to be here. I wanted to shout at the passage of time that made all of my kids closer to moving away from home.

So, this year was harder than usual. I had a good cry during my devotions on the morning of Daniel's birthday and realized how so many things changed on that day. I was afraid for his safety on the road and my inability to protect him. I was sad that as he grows older, he would need me less often and for fewer things. I was worried that I just won't see him enough and that I have now lost the time we used to have in the car. I was being called upon to be a different kind of mom.

I would have loved to have a family "blessing of the keys" to mark this transition (something a friend did with the youth at the congregation she served). But I was aware that I needed this and Daniel did not. I took my cues from him and blessed the keys in the quiet of the morning before he rose and drove away.

Being Laid Bare

If you want to discover all of your faults, weaknesses, blind spots, and unresolved emotional issues, I would recommend having children. Being a parent lays you bare like no other experience in life (and I have done a lot of therapy and spiritual direction). Since I became a mom, I have felt ecstatic joy and delight beyond imagining, as well as the grip of sheer terror and the despair of complete helplessness. Every day, I bump up against my limitations—the mom I imagine myself to be and the mom I really am.

I worked desperately to make my children happy, only to have a child psychologist tell me that was not my job; he encouraged me instead to help them cope with the disappointments and vagaries of life with resilience. This left me wondering how I could be so stupid, and later, wondering why I was still trying to make them happy.

While visiting our new neighbors, an Orthodox Jewish Rabbi and his wife, I heard Jacob swear when he spilled his juice. He repeated a short phrase he heard me whisper under my breath in exasperation. After mortal embarrassment, it bonded us as friends for life (they have four children, so they understood!).

I encouraged my children to express their feelings and then sometimes found myself pining for the days when children were "seen but not heard." I tried to talk openly about all the issues of life, only to discover later that I had missed a window of important conversation on more than one occasion.

Admitting limitation and weakness was difficult for me, but as a parent, my flaws became unavoidably glaring. There was so much I could not control. When I was a child, my parents encouraged me "to do my best." I didn't know that my best might be different every day depending on what was happening and how I was feeling. Somewhere in my little brain, "doing my best" became conflated with "being the best" and a perfectionist was born. I equated self-esteem with self-confidence and I created the latter through accomplishments with the ultimate hope of earning love and approval. It wasn't until much later that I realized that self-esteem comes from "being-ness" and not "doing-ness," but it was difficult to let go of the pattern of trying to earn love that was already freely given.

In my twenties, I finally began to develop a positive self-image apart from achievement or doing something for others; I slowly embraced a sense of self, rooted in being created by a loving God. The feeling of hyper-responsibility, however, has never gone away completely. I have no doubt that my parents have always loved me no matter what; when I became a parent, I struggled to find a way to communicate this unconditional love to my children, while at the same time, holding up the importance of making their best effort.

So I developed a morning ritual when the kids went off to school. As they trundled out the door, backs slumped against the weight of backpacks, I always said, "You are lovable, capable, and valuable and I believe in you, so make it a great day! I love you!" When I tucked them in at night, I would say, "I love you no matter what, and I am proud of you for ... (fill in the blank from the day). I prayed that my unconditional love would encourage self-esteem arising from just being who they were, and my pride at their accomplishments would develop self-confidence in what they could do.

Over time, the bedside conversation faded as they no longer wanted or needed to be tucked in. But every single day, even in high school, I still sent them off with the same ritual, "You are lovable, capable, and valuable and I believe in you, so make it a great day! I love you!" Sometimes it felt stupid or silly to all of us. But they accepted that this was just what Mom says, while maybe secretly wishing I wouldn't say it in front of their friends during carpool. I said it anyway.

Did this ritual help them develop both self-esteem and self-confidence? I'm not completely sure. Perhaps it was more about me trying to make sure they knew how much I loved them, even when I flunked, even in the moments when I was far from the mom I imagined I should be, and even when I was tripped up by my own limitations and weaknesses.

We did receive a glimpse of the impact of my daily affirmation when we moved Daniel to college for his freshman year. Dan and I stood in the parking lot to say good-bye and drive away. I hugged Daniel close, then looked him in the eyes and through tears, I said, "You are loveable, capable, and valuable, and I believe in you, so make it a great day! I love you!" Both Daniel and Dan cried, too, and suddenly this little ritual took on a larger meaning:

Daniel had heard this about 2,300 times before and now it was time to say it for himself.

I cried for a long time after we drove away. I felt a physical ache in my gut that urged every cell in my body to turn around and go back. Had I been driving, we would have turned around. But Dan drove and he said, "no" as kindly as he could every time I told him we absolutely had to turn around. Daniel had graduated from high school a year early and I was out of time to make up for my mistakes. It was time for me trust at an even deeper level that God would love Daniel and be with him no matter what.

When it was time to send Jacob off to college, I had to say goodbye at the airport. This was a painful choice, but Dan had the necessary muscles needed for moving; I was hampered by too many upper body surgeries to be of much help, so practicality won out. Through tears, I offered my same affirmation, "Jacob, you are lovable, capable and valuable, and I believe in you, so make it a great day! I love you!" I cried and drove myself home, praying for God to be with him and for me to trust enough to let go.

I still have a year before Leah goes off to college and I am not looking forward to that empty-nest farewell. But you can bet that whether she's embarrassed or not, she will hear my ritual affirmation every day of her senior year. I pray it's enough love to cover my faults and to last a lifetime.

The Excruciating and the Sacred

T he last day with my mom was both excruciating and sacred. With my dad's attention and care, she had lived a surprising three years after her initial diagnosis of liver disease. But she contracted a MRSA infection (staph that is antibiotic resistant) that she could not fight off. My sister, brother, and I flew from Wisconsin, California, and Missouri to join our other sister and Dad, who lived in the Dallas-Fort Worth area of Texas.

After a few days of hoping and praying for a different outcome, the five of us gathered around Mom's bed in the ICU. It was time to remove the machines and turn down the medicine that was keeping her alive. The pain was deep and multifaceted, profound and crushing. I did not want to let her go, yet it was distressing to see her suffer. I wanted time to stop and hold the sweep of death at bay; hold the infection back so we could keep her a little longer.

But she was the one who was holding—holding on for us—showing strength that we did not fathom she had, revealing a depth of wisdom and patience we could only see after she passed over. Mom endured pain and suffering while we struggled, cried, prayed, accepted, and as much as we could, got ready. She had been ready. She was waiting for us. Mom was holding on to the thread of life, the thread of love, the thread that binds us one to another, taking care of us as only a mom can. Mom held on and waited for our readiness to the very end despite liver disease, mental confusion, and physical distress. This was both a salve for my soul and an excruciating realization; I was in awe of this marvelous person I have called Mom for forty-nine years.

How many are given this gift of truly seeing in death, the whole depth, scope, and meaning of a person's life? It is a sacred space, where time opens up and offers her gifts. The veil separating this life from the next becomes a thin, luminescent space filled with the holy presence of God in the intermingling of death and life, strength and sorrow, courage and loss.

We were there, in that sacred space, finally with words of acceptance and permission. Her pastor led us in a Service of Forgiveness and Commendation as we entered into her dying process. We sang her favorite hymns and recited familiar Bible passages. Through tears, we named the relatives and saints who would welcome her into heaven as her body gave way, and Mom took her last breath.

"No!" was the first word uttered. We cried, "no" against the cavernous loss. God's holy hand held Mom, and gently said, "Yes." Yes to her. Yes to us. Yes to life in the fluttering of the liminal veil.

Acknowledgments

This book would never have become a reality without my writing teacher and coach, Bobbi Linkemer. It was a blessed day when I walked into a community-education class at our high school to learn about writing a nonfiction book! She has been a friend and champion ever since, and went above and beyond in every way to make sure my writing was published. Bobbi did everything humanly possible for me, including editing it twice, getting that darn proposal written while I was receiving chemo treatments for breast cancer, and connecting me to an incredible copyeditor, Jody Amato; a wonderful publisher, Kira Henschel at HenschelHAUS Publishing; and a creative book designer, Peggy Nehmen of Nehmen-Kodner Graphic Design. I am indebted to you, Bobbi, and so grateful for your wisdom, friendship, and all your hard work on my behalf!

Jody, you were the first person to whom I entrusted my book; your unbiased feedback and encouragement were invaluable in keeping me going. You also made my writing better than it was before—thank you!

Kira, I don't know how you do what you do, but it's been an adventure and delight to work on this process with you! Thank you for your guidance, flexibility, and profes-sionalism.

Peggy, you are an attentive listener, creative worker, and helped me think about book design in the larger context of marketing, giving me much more than I ever imagined. Thank you for your energy and beautiful work in helping make this dream come true.

Special thanks to Karen Hilmes and Otto Schultejans. Our small writing group at the beginning of this process was invaluable and kept me writing so I had something to read every time we met. I'm so grateful for your time and support.

Other family and friends encouraged me along the way, especially my dad, Roger Anderson, and my siblings, Doug Anderson, Pam Otto, and Julie Emmett. My sister-in-law, Alice Grevet, has designed two blogs for me since I started writing and given me beautiful platforms to share my musings. I am indebted you, Alice, for all your time and skill!

The love and interest of the rest of our extended family prodded me to keep writing down what my children said and did, so I could send out periodic emails updating everyone on their comments and antics; without their loving interest, I may not have kept such an accurate record of these stories.

In addition, I owe my sanity to my dear friends, Susan Candea, Kendra Nolde, Joan Wysession, and Karen Trenne, who laughed and cried with me over the years. I am especially grateful to Susan Candea, who helped me send off the first submissions to a few publishers and then, two years ago at a feminist conference we attended, encouraged me to get this dream off the shelf. Thank you all for believing in me.

I hold deep gratitude for the members of the congregations Dan and I have served, who embraced our children as their own family, including St. Mark's Hope and Peace Lutheran and Covenant Presbyterian churches in Kansas City, Missouri; St. Mark's Lutheran Church in Clayton, Missouri; and most of all, Trinity Presbyterian Church in University City, Missouri, which provided an incredible home for our children as they grew up. My children are so fortunate to have had an abundance of wise and faithful adults nurturing their spirits.

This book wouldn't exist without my three amazing and interesting children: Leah, Jacob, and Daniel. I continue to learn and grow through your presence in my life. Thank you for letting me share some of your stories, your humor, your insights, and your character with others. You have given me one of life's greatest gifts, which is to help me see and experience the presence of the sacred within our life together. My daily life has become sacramental because you are in it. I'm so happy God let me be your mom.

Finally, I'm grateful to my husband, Dan, who has encouraged me to write, edited my essays, shared my writing with others, made suggestions, and helped create space for me to write, especially on our family trips to Ghost Ranch. You are a great dad, a wonderful life partner, and even though I still don't know why you love me, I am so blessed you do. Thank you for sharing the adventure of life, parenting, family, and ministry with me.

ABout the Author

The Reverend Linda Anderson-Little was ordained a pastor in the Evangelical Lutheran Church in America (ELCA) in 1989. She has served congregations in Detroit, Michigan, as well as Kansas City and Clayton, Missouri. Linda was a stay-at-home mom for nine years while her children were small, and ran a home-based business. During this time, she reflected on her spiritual experiences in family life through writing essays, which led to this book.

Currently, Linda serves as the Interim Associate Pastor at Lutheran Church of the Atonement in Florissant, Missouri, blogs at soulstorywriter.net, and is pursuing a Certificate in Spiritual Direction at the Aquinas Institutes of Theology. She lives in St. Louis, Missouri.

Contact Linda through social media:
Email through website: http://soulstorywriter.net
Twitter: @SoulStoryLinda
Facebook: https://www.facebook.com/linda.andersonlittle
LinkedIn: https://www.linkedin.com/in/linda-anderson-little